Geraint Bowen

WELSH RECUSANT WRITINGS

University of Wales Press

Cardiff 1999

I

The term 'recusant' was originally used in registering Roman Catholics who refused to attend Anglican services in parish churches as required by law during the reign of Elizabeth, the Protestant queen. But some papists unwilling to conform with the Act of Uniformity had fled the country before the Privy Council requested bishops to compile the register; their names do not appear on these lists. Neither do the names of secular priests who returned on secret missions, some of them martyrs; nor the names of covert papists or Catholic sympathizers who outwardly conformed, some of them in order to avoid costly punishment, such as fines and loss of property. Several registered recusants as well as some whose names do not appear on these legal documents made a contribution to Welsh recusant writings. In this respect we use the term 'recusant writings' to mean 'writings by Catholics from all groups, open or covert'. These writings are not necessarily writings on Catholic devotions and dogma or in defence of papal supremacy or other specifically Catholic matters. If one were to confine oneself in this treatise to dealing with such works, one would exclude discussion of some of the most important contributions by Catholics to the Welsh scholarship and literature of the Tudor period. In fact the Catholic émigrés were the first to make such contributions.

Morys Clynnog, secretary and chancellor to Cardinal Pole at Lambeth Palace during Queen Mary's reign and the bishop elect of Bangor, Gruffydd Robert, archdeacon of Anglesey, Owen Lewis, a lecturer in law at Oxford, Thomas Goldwell, bishop of St Asaph who had also been in the service of Pole, and probably Siôn Dafydd Rhys, a student of Christ Church, Oxford, all left the country at different times between 1557 and 1563, the year of the enthronement of Elizabeth, and settled in Louvain in the Low Countries where most of the English Catholic refugees had established themselves. In the early 1560s the Welsh émigrés moved to northern Italy and later to Rome, Goldwell to become *custos* of the English Pilgrim Hospice and later vicar-general to Carlo Borromeo. Morys Clynnog replaced Goldwell as *custos* and Gruffydd Robert was appointed chaplain at the Hospice. When the Hospice was converted into a seminary to be known as the Seminarium Anglicum, Morys Clynnog was appointed rector. About the same time Owen Lewis, who had been appointed canon of Cambrai and archdeacon of Hainault, moved to Rome, having been given the key position of *referendarius*, the Pope's adviser on English political and religious matters.

Carlo Borromeo, the nephew of Pius IV, pope from 1559 to 1565, was archbishop of Milan and chairman of the Ecumenical Council of Trent for a time. This Council was opened in 1545 by Pope Paul III and aimed at the purgation of the Church and the strengthening of papal authority. It declared that scripture alone, *sola scriptura*, was not the only rule of faith as the Lutherans or Protestants claimed and that Church customs transmitted from apostolic times were also to be accepted and revered. Jerome's Latin Bible, the Vulgate, was to be the authoritative version of the scriptures, and public devotions in churches were to be held without exception in the Latin tongue throughout Christendom. The various articles of faith were clarified, and Carlo Borromeo was the prime mover in producing the CATECHISMUS ROMANUS in 1566. Borromeo resided in the papal palace in Rome during the time Pius IV held office. At the death of the Pope he returned to Milan, but in the interim a special relationship had grown between him and Gruffydd Robert, which resulted in Gruffydd Robert being appointed his personal confessor.

Carlo Borromeo was not only the leader of Catholic reform, but also an exponent of Renaissance learning, and during his chairmanship of the Council of Trent the assembly declared that the teaching of Aristotle and humanist concepts had equal authority to the decrees of the Catholic Church in matters of dogma. The papal palace in Rome and the archbishop's court in Milan, mainly owing to the influence of Carlo Borromeo, were seats of humanist thought and the meeting places of committed humanists. Undoubtedly his personal relationship with the humanist Borromeo had its effect on Gruffydd Robert. It enriched him with the knowledge and enthusiasm that enabled him to become an expounder of Aristotelianism to the Welsh. But Gruffydd Robert was convinced that the Welsh language in its current state was incapacitated by the lack of standardization of orthography and was bereft of the vocabulary and refinement of expression necessary to enable a Welshman to define humanism either in original Welsh writings or in translations from Greek and Latin humanist works.

Many authors in the university cities of northern Italy, such as Bologna, Florence, Milan, Padua, Pistoia and Siena, with their wealthy patrons of classical art, had sought to refine the prevailing Tuscan or Florentian vernacular of their patrons as a worthy literary medium. The poet Dante (1255–1321) in his book DE VULGARI ELOQUENTIA had made a case for the use of Tuscan, and Pietro Bembo (1470–1547) followed his lead with his PROSE DELLA VOLGAR LINGUA (1525), and Benedetto Varchi with L'ERCOLANO (1560). The University of Bologna, established in the eleventh century, had been attended by such Renaissance writers as Dante and Petrarch in their student days, and in recognition of its academic potential, Carlo Borromeo in 1562 by order of Pius IV had provided the university with a new building. Other famous advocates of Tuscan had been professors or *alumni* at Padua University. These included Bembo, Giulio Cesare Scaligero (1484–1558), Sperone Speroni (1500–1588), a strong advocate for the use of the vernacular, Bernardo Tasso (1493–1569), and the Aristotelian Pietro Pomponazzi (1462–1525).

The innovation and the development of printing, however, brought pressure on philologists to standardize the Tuscan orthography. The classical scholar Francesco Fortunio, in his REGOLE GRAMMATICALLI DELLA VOLGAR LINGUA (1516), provided the guidelines to uniformity, and his suggestions gained popularity as a result of the publication of the works of the prolific classicist Giangiorgio Trissino (1478–1550), which included plays, Homeric poems and numerous translations in the new orthography. In 1548 Bernardo Segni's translation of Aristotle's POETICO, a work that was frequently read publicly at Padua University, appeared in print. Indeed

Aristotle by this time dominated the Tuscan literary scene, and Scaligero in his exposition of the works of Aristotle, POETICES LIBRI SEPTEM, referred to him as *Aristotles imperator noster, omnium artium dictator perpetuus* ('Aristotle is our emperor, the universal dictator of all art'). He insisted that Tuscan authors should follow Aristotle's rationalist way of thinking and imitate the epideictic style of classical authors like Cicero. Only thus could the spoken language of Tuscany be updated and become an effective and acceptable literary medium, and writing an artistic pursuit.

Siôn Dafydd Rhys, who had followed his compatriots to Italy, settled in Pistoia as tutor to the children of Vicenzo Gheri, the brother of Filippo Gheri, bishop of Ischia. He later enrolled as a student of medicine at Siena University, graduating in 1567. Whilst resident at Pistoia he completed and published a Greek grammar written in Latin and a small Latin grammar in the Tuscan vernacular, REGOLE DELLA CONSTRUTTIONE LATINA, which was printed in Venice in 1567. The frequent references to Morys Clynnog in this volume suggest that Clynnog was regarded by Siôn Dafydd Rhys as his patron. Undoubtedly this publication was sufficient proof of his mastery of the classics and the local vernacular, a qualification that gained the approval of the local renaissance circle of philologists and patrons of literature. These philologists included Orazio Lombardelli, author of DELLA PRONUNZIO TOSCANA (1568), Claudio Tolomei (1492–1555), who had argued strongly for the use of Tuscan in his books IL CESANO and IL POLITA, and Pier Franceso Giambullari, author of DE LA LINGUA CHE SI PARLA E SCRIVE IN FIRENZE (1551).

In 1569 Siôn Dafydd Rhys published another book, a Latin guide to the pronunciation of Italian, PERVTILIS EXTERIS NATIONIBVS DE ITALICA PRONUNCIATIONE & ORTHOGRAPHIA LIBELLUS, which he dedicated to his *patronus* and *Maecenas* Robert Peccham, a Catholic refugee, son of Sir Edward Peccham, former member of the Privy Council. In it he compares the pronunciation and orthography of Tuscan with that of Welsh, English, French, Spanish, Portuguese, German and Polish. Siôn Dafydd Rhys was not the first Welshman to publish a manual on Italian. William Thomas, prebend of St Paul's, London, and member of the Privy Council during the reign of the Protestant King Edward VI, compiled and published in 1550 PRINCIPAL RULES OF THE ITALIAN GRAMMER WITH A DICTIONARIE FOR THE BETTER UNDERSTANDYNGE OF BOCCACE, PETRARCHE AND DANTE; he was exiled and lived amongst philologists in Padua and Bologna, and was later executed for treason in 1554. In his volume DE ITALICA PRONUNCIATIONE Siôn Dafydd Rhys pays tribute in verse to two Latin scholars with whom he was acquainted, the Frenchman Rinaldus Molinetta and the Portuguese Francisco De Brito. He also makes specific reference to Gruffydd Robert's newly printed Welsh grammar and also to Morys Clynnog's catechism, which is evidence that he was familiar with these works before he returned to Wales in 1571.

In Gruffydd Robert's opinion Welsh literature was in an impoverished state, as there were no Welsh translations of classical literary works. No attempt had ever been made to provide what he describes as knowledge about things and deeds worth knowing about. He was of the opinion that this was not attainable without a class of patrons like those whom he had known in Italy and those who had ensured the success of Renaissance learning in Spain and France. But even without that support he was prepared to do what he could to adapt the Welsh language to Renaissance needs.

The first essential in his view was a Welsh grammar. He compiled such a work while he was serving as chaplain in the Pilgrim Hospice in Rome and after associating with men of letters and leaders of renaissance thought like Carlo Borromeo and reading their works. The introductory parts of the grammar describe in ornate Ciceronian style a hot summer scene in a Roman vineyard, contrasting it with a scene in Wales, and reveal his longing for his homeland and his love for his kinsmen. This love for country, he explained, made one talk about Welsh matters and what could be done to improve them. Classical authors when in similar retreats would write about the things that would improve the cultural lives of their fellow men, as Cicero had done. But, he maintained, although one could not compete with such men of genius and produce comparable works, nevertheless such works could be translated as had been done in Italy, France and Spain. But the Welsh language did not have the necessary vocabulary, and it lacked refinement *yn brin ei geiriau, er bod yr iaith ohoni ei hun cyn gyfoethoced ag un arall* ('lacking in its words, although the language itself is as richly endowed as any other'). If one wanted the Welsh language to develop into a refined literary medium, the first essential requirement was a grammar.

The grammar DOSPARTH BYRR AR Y RHANN GYNTAF I RAMADEG CYMRAEG was published by Vicenzo

Girardoni in Milan in 1567 (with additions in 1584 and 1594). Copies of the printed book are known to have reached the homeland in 1567. One of the copies preserved at the National Library of Wales carries the mark of ownership of John Dee and the date 1567. As in classical works such as Plato's, Gruffydd Robert's grammar is composed in the form of a dialogue, *ymddiddan deuddyn* (discourse between two persons). It takes the form of a discussion between the author and Morys Clynnog. The first part deals comprehensively with phonology, orthography and pronunciation, and the second part with accidence, punctuation and rules for borrowing words from Latin and Greek and even from English, *phord deg, a guedaid i uneuthur gair ladin yn gamraegaid pan fo eisio gair cyfattebaul, i'r ladin, ne i'r Groeg* (p. 194) ('a fine and neat way of changing a Latin word into Welsh whenever a Welsh word like in sense to a Latin or Greek word is required'), with additional sections dealing with the traditional bardic art, *cynghanedd* and metrics. He rarely elaborates on mutations and syntax, arguing that Welsh speakers knew instinctively how to formulate sentences: *e dysg dyn gystrauenu'r geiriau cymraeg yn gynt, urth i glust, a hir dall ar yr iaith, nog urth reolaethau' celfydyd* (pp. 206–7) ('a person learns Welsh syntax sooner by listening and by long acquaintance with the language than by the rules of the art').

As the above quotations indicate, there are some novel suggestions in his grammar that make manifest the state of Welsh orthography in the sixteenth century, for example the letters *d, l, u,* and *ph* should be substituted for *dd, ll, w* and *ff* and the letter *c* used for *k*; the initial letters of proper nouns should be capitals; words like *ymhlith* should be written as uttered *ymlhith*, and *yn nhy* as *ynnhy*; the final consonants in monosyllabic words with short vowels should not be doubled (*gwen* not *gwenn*); the definite article should be attached to pronouns (*yrhwn*, *yrhain*); the possessive pronoun *fy* joined to the noun that follows (*pen / fymhen*); a preposition attached to a pronoun (*atafinnau*); and the personal pronoun attached to the verb (*gwelwchwi*). As no Welsh grammar had been published previously, Gruffydd Robert was obliged to coin new grammatical terms. The following examples appear in the First Part: *ailflaenllym* (acute accent on penult), *ailgymedrol* (circumflex accent on the penult) and *blaenbwl* (grave accent).

In his section on the Latin element in Welsh, he makes no reference to vowel and dipthong changes, but we do find numerous words that he coined from Latin: *dogfen < documentum, siampl < exemplum*. His guidance on the formation of abstract nouns and his suggestions for new Welsh formations such as *amodol, bygythiol, cyfansoddol, genedigol, gostegol* etc. were intended to assist translators of classical works. Many of his original formations went into common use.

His description of the *cynganeddion* is unsatisfactory. He fails to make reference to the accent of words, an indispensable element in the understanding and practice of the traditional bardic art. His commentary on the strict metres is also faulty. In Professor G. J. Williams's view, *He knew very little about the metres*. But Gruffydd Robert was quick to defend himself in the opening words of this section by explaining that the poets kept the secrets of their poetic art to themselves and only disclosed them to novitiates, and that some other person more qualified than himself in this matter should take on the task of instructing the intelligent, the religious and the gifted in the correct way of composing poems in the traditional manner. He explains also that some poets prefer free verse and emphasizes that the strict metres are not suitable for long poems. In his view, rhyming couplets, as practised by the Italian poets, or carol metres should be adopted, and others invented. He provides examples of these metrical forms, and to illustrate classical prose at its elegant best he publishes his translation of Cicero's essay DE SENECTUTE (*On Old Age*).

It appears that Gruffydd Robert had begun to practise his skill in the traditional poetic art before he emigrated, as some of his religious compositions in metrical forms appear in Welsh manuscripts written about 1563–5. Later they were included in a booklet printed probably in a secret press and entitled YNGLYNION AR Y PADER, Y CREDO, AC AR DEG GORCHYMYN O WAITH D:G:R: YR ATHRAW MAWR O DRE FULAN ('*Englynion* on the Lord's Prayer, the Creed, and on the Ten Commandments by Doctor Gruffydd Robert, the great scholar from Milan'). These appeared amended in the anthology of verse in the grammar with the title SYMBLEN YR ABOSTOLION, A EILU'R CYMRU, Y GREDO, A DEUDEG PRIFBUNC YNDI, UEDI I CYNNUYS MEUN DEUDEG ENGLYN ('The Apostolic Creed, called by the Welsh, *y gredo*, and the twelve main articles contained in it, composed into twelve *englynion*'). These compositions are in the strict metres, and deal with the Apostolic Creed, The Lord's Prayer, The Angelical Salutation (Ave Maria), The Ten Commandments, The Sacraments (baptism, confirmation, eucharist, penitence, unction,

marriage and ordination) and The Eight Beatitudes.
His first *englyn* reads as follows:

> *I'r tad yn ụastad, estyd, y credaf,*
>   *creaudr dibạl hyfryd:*
>   *a ụnaeth y nenn uụch benn byd*
>   *hoeụfaith a'r ḍaear hefyd.* (p. 333)

*(I always diligently believe in the Father, the eternal, blessed
creator, who made the long-lasting and ever active heaven above
and also the earth.)*

The anthology also includes *cywyddau* by two
medieval poets, Siôn Cent and Dafydd ap Gwilym,
others by two contemporary poets, Gruffudd Hir-
aethog and Siôn Tudur, and two exemplar *cywyddau*
on the Psalms of David by Gruffydd Robert himself,
followed by a glossary of his newly coined Latin-
derived words as used in his religious *cywyddau*. By
publishing this anthology he confirmed that his
grammar was intended as a means of enriching the
Welsh language as a literary medium for prose
writers in general, but first and foremost for poets to
excel in composing religious and meaningful
cywyddau in praise of God and the benefit of the
human soul, *mal y gallo pob gụr dysgedig, duụiol,
auenyḍus gael cyfaruydḍid i uneuthur cannigion a
chouyddau santeiḍiol a rhinuedol* (p. 208) ('so that every
learned, religious and gifted person be taught how
to compose religious and pious verses and
cywyddau').

The first Catholic publication to be influenced by
Gruffydd Robert's work was Morys Clynnog's
Welsh translation of Ioannes Polanco's DE DOCTRINA
CHRISTIANA, namely ATHRAVAETH GRISTNOGAVL. The

only extant copy is kept in the Newberry Library, Chicago. Polanco, a Jesuit theologian, was born at Burgos in Spain in 1517. He became the first secretary general of the Jesuit Society and lived in Rome, where he died in 1574. He was a prolific writer, publishing at least eleven books, one of them, the DE DOCTRINA CHRISTIANA, anonymously. Polanco is known to be the author because Owen Lewis, in a letter dated 1579 to the Vatican Librarian, Cardinal Sirleto, mentions that no Welsh Catholic book other than Morys Clynnog's translation of Polanco's catechism had ever been published.

Morys Clynnog sent a draft of his translation to Gruffydd Robert, who had by now settled in Milan. Gruffydd Robert was so glad to receive such a treasure in the Welsh language that he decided to publish it: *e lauenychod fynghalon urth ueled tryssor mor urthfaur yn yr iaith gymraeg . . . ni elais ar fynghalon na pharun i brintio* ('my heart rejoiced at the sight of so valuable a treasure in the Welsh language that I really could not do other than arrange for it to be printed'). He edited the draft and published it in Milan in 1568. The woodcut on the title-page, apart from the encompassing *englyn*, is identical with that on another book published by Vicenzo Girardoni, the printer of the Welsh grammar. The published book bears the obvious impress of Gruffydd Robert's recommendations. In the preamble, which opens with the words *Gruphyd fab Rhobert yn annerch yr hyparch brelad a'i dibal gynheiliad M. Morys Clynoc* ('Gruffydd fab Rhobert addressing the venerable prelate and his unfailing patron M. Morys Clynoc'), he assumes that the catechism is Clynnog's original work and expresses the hope that he will have the strength to produce more works for the benefit of

Christians and the glory of God, *nerth i chuithau i scrifennu chuaneg er les i'r Cristnogion a gogoniant i dduu.*

The contents (*Y pynciav hynottaf*·), the preface (*Rhaglith*) with its verses in strict metres and Welsh translations of extracts from St John Chrysostom's Homilies are most likely Gruffydd Robert's work. Morys Clynnog's translation follows in the accepted catechismal pattern of the period and deals with the name Christian, the sign of the cross, man's destination, the apostolic creed, hope, the Lord's Prayer, Ave Maria, praying to saints, charity, good deeds, the Decalogue, the precepts of the Church, the sacraments, the eight beatitudes and the mysteries in Christ's life. As an addendum, an index to the contents is provided to assist preachers, together with a list of misprints and a glossary of Latin derivatives.

The printed text is throughout in Gruffydd Robert's orthography in all its detail. This unique orthography had required the printer to cast special fonts for the printing of the grammar, and Vicenzo Girardoni's press was the obvious choice for the publishing of the catechism too. The numerous Latin borrowings used reflect those found in Gruffydd Robert's grammar. But there are also many not found in the grammar, nor in any earlier Welsh texts, such as *cymgadwriaeth* ('continentia'), *dirgeledd* ('mysterium') and *goddefedd* ('patientia'). These may have been Morys Clynnog's own creations or Gruffydd Robert's attempts to amend the text. A personal letter written in Welsh by Morys Clynnog to Sir William Cecil in 1567 proves that Clynnog willingly accepted Gruffydd Robert's guidance on orthography, but however much editing can be attributed to Gruffydd Robert, we have to accept that the original draft of the translation was the work of Morys Clynnog.

Gruffydd Robert promised Morys Clynnog that he would send printed copies to Wales immediately, and there is evidence that he kept his promise. Lewis Evans of Gwent, once a Catholic refugee and later a turncoat to Protestantism, published in 1571 a criticism of the catechism in a book entitled A BRIEF ANSWER TO A SMALL TRIFLING TREATISE OF LATE SET FORTH IN THE BRITAINE TONGUE WRITTEN BY ONE CLINNOCK AT ROME, AND PRINTED AT MILLAIN, AND LATELY SPREAD SECRETLY ABROAD IN WALES. Unfortunately all copies of this book have disappeared.

In the letter previously referred to, which Owen Lewis submitted to Cardinal Sirleto in 1579 pleading for financial support for the printing of Welsh religious books, he mentions the names of three Welsh texts that had already been prepared for the press, giving the titles in Latin: DE ECCLESIA ET PRIMATIS R PONTIFICIS (*Concerning the Church and the Supremacy of the Pope of Rome*), DE SACRAMENTO ET SACRIFICIO ALTARIS (*Concerning the Sacrament and the Eucharist*) and CATECHISMI P. CANICIJ VERSORUM IN LINGUAM BRITANNICAM (*The Catechism of Father Canisius translated into Welsh*). He also states that it was his intention to publish them in Milan under the editorship and supervision of Gruffydd Robert. The plea for aid came to nothing. But this ambitious scheme is evidence of a determination by the Welsh émigrés in Italy to serve their country well.

It may be that the translation of the catechism was the work of Rhosier Smyth of St Asaph, who had graduated at Oxford in 1563 and in 1576 taken refuge as a student in the seminary in Douai, Brabant. In 1579, accompanied by Morgan Clynnog, the nephew of Morys Clynnog, he came to Rome and registered as a student in the Seminarium Anglicum. When the seminary authorities under the influence of the Jesuits declared, against Morys Clynnog's will, that all its students had to make a vow that they intended to return on the English mission, Rhosier Smyth refused and left. Another student, Huw Griffith, a nephew of Owen Lewis, although he agreed, was dismissed. After much discord Morys Clynnog was also obliged to resign. He left for France and later by ship for Spain. The ship was wrecked and he was drowned.

Both Smyth and Griffith were befriended by Owen Lewis, a known opponent of the Jesuits, a friendship that lasted till the death of Lewis. Smyth remained in Italy and continued his studies, graduating as Doctor of Divinity and opting for ordination. In 1580 Owen Lewis moved to Milan as vicar-general to Carlo Borromeo, and in 1588 he was consecrated bishop of Cassano; he was later appointed papal nuncio to Switzerland, returning to Rome where he died in 1595. Rhosier Smyth returned to England and was imprisoned. He reports thus: *I was taken and put into Newgate where, I protest, I did expect nothing but death but that God did then provide the better friend for me and by that means delivered.* Gruffydd Robert had heard of his experience and wrote him a letter of congratulation: *I am glad that you succeeded in picking the locks of Newgate* ('Mae'n dda gennyf fedru ohonot bigo cloeau Neugat'). The close relationship that had grown between Owen Lewis and Rhosier Smyth leads one to believe that the translation of Canisius's catechism referred to in Lewis's letter to Sirleto was one and the same as Rhosier Smyth's translation of the catechism, which was later published in Paris.

Rhosier Smyth did not return to Rome but took up residence in Rouen and later in Paris. He was introduced to and gained the patronage of Jacques Davy Duperron, bishop of Evreux, the leader of the Counter-Reformation in France. Duperron published numerous works, some of which were translated into English. It was with his support that Smyth after years of frustration succeeded in publishing his translation of Canisius' catechism. It appears that Duperron knew nothing of the existence of the Welsh nation, and Smyth had to explain to him that a part of 'England' was inhabited by a nation different from the English, that this nation was the first in Europe to embrace the Faith and that a different language was spoken by this nation and very little English was understood.

The first edition of Canisius's SUMMA DOCTRINAE CHRISTIANAE (*Catechismus Major*) had appeared in 1555. This was followed by smaller editions, CATECHISMUS MINOR and CATECHISMUS MINIMUS. An English translation of CATECHISMUS MINOR was published in 1579 and Henry Garnet's translation of CATECHISMUS MAJOR sometime around 1592–6, having been printed by a secret press in London. The catechisms were translated into most of the languages of Europe. Smyth refers to the fact that even a Breton translation had already been printed, referring to CATECHISM HAC INSTRUCTION . . . COMPOSET EN LATIN GANT M.P. CANISIUS . . . UES A SOCIETE AN HANU JESUS (Paris, 1576). Two editions of Rhosier Smyth's free translation and, in parts, a summary, were published, according to the press mark, in Paris, the first in 1609 entitled CRYNNODEB O ADDYSG CRIST-NOGAWL . . . GWEDI GYFIAITHU O'R LADIN I'R GYMERAEG DRWY DDYFAL ASTUDIAETH A LLAFUR D. ROSIER SMYTH O DREF LLANELWY, and the second, an enlarged edition, in 1611 with the title OPUS CATECHISTICUM . . . SEF YV SVM, NE GRYNODEB O ADDYSG GRISTIONOGAVL . . . A GYFIAITHWYD O'R LADIN I'R GYMRAEG DRVY DDYFAL LAFYR AG ASTUDIAETH D. ROSIER SMYTH O DREF LLANELVY. In the preface he complains about the condition of Welsh orthography and states that he had thought it wise to follow Gruffydd Robert's recommendations, similarly formulating essential words from Latin. According to THE UNIVERSITY OF WALES DICTIONARY (*Geiriadur Prifysgol Cymru*), Welsh root words that he coined are numerous, for example, *aflonyddus, astudiaeth, arweiniwr*.

It appears that Rhosier Smyth chose to translate the work of Canisius following the declaration of Emperor Ferdinand prohibiting the use of any other catechism in the schools in his empire. Philip, King of Spain, had also issued an edict to the same effect. There were also other possible reasons. It was the only catechism studied at the Catholic seminary at Douai where Smyth had been a student, and probably the only catechism that Duperron, his patron, was ready to sponsor. There was also a desperate need in Wales for a catechism, forty years having gone by since the publication of ATHRAVAETH GRISTNOGAVL.

In 1612 Rhosier Smyth also published in the city of Paris on the last day of October (*yn Ninas Paris, dydd diwaethaf o fis Hydref M.DC.XII*), a book entitled COPPI O LYTHYR CREFYDHWR A MERTHYR DEDHFOL

DYSCEDIG AT I DAD IW GYNGHORI I 'MWRTHOD AG
OFEREDH A GWAGEDH Y BYD AG I FEDHWL AM Y ENAID, a
translation of Robert Southwell's EPISTLE OF A
RELIGIOUS PRIEST VNTO HIS FATHER: EXORTING HIM TO THE
PERFECT FORSAKING OF THE WORLD. TO THE VORSHIPFVL,
HIS VERY GOOD FATHER, R.S. HIS DUETIFULL SONNE R.S.
WISHETH ALL HAPPINESSE. In this translation Rhosier
Smyth rejects some of the features of Gruffydd
Robert's orthography and adopts in part the
orthography that Siôn Dafydd Rhys used in his
grammar, INSTITUTIONES (1592), using *dh* for *dd* and *lh*
for *ll*. He continues to use *ph* for *ff*, and as *w* was not
available in French presses, he used *vv* instead.

Robert Southwell (1561–1595) was a Jesuit priest who
had returned from exile in 1586 and had sought in vain
to make contact with his father Richard Southwell,
who had during his son's absence abroad conformed
and was employed in the royal court. It was on 22
October 1589, some years after he had been disowned
by his family and after his appointment as secret
confessor to Anne Howard, the wife of the Earl of
Arundel, that Southwell wrote the letter to his father.

William Allen had instructed students at Douai to
write letters home to their parents in order to restore
them to the Catholic faith. These circulated amongst
relatives and friends, and some of them were
printed. Robert Southwell's letter was printed at
least five times, the first time on the occasion of his
martyrdom in 1597. He was one of the hundred or
more Catholic priests who were martyred during the
reign of Elizabeth.

The Welsh translation is dedicated to Morgan
Clynnog, who was Smyth's fellow student at the

Seminarium Anglicum and who had returned to Wales in 1582 as a secular missionary priest, serving mainly in Carmarthenshire and Glamorgan and dwelling in the home of the Turberville family in Pen-llin. In his address he thanks Morgan Clynnog for sending him a copy of the original printed text (of 52 pages). Having read it, he had decided to translate it, because, he adds:

Every man who reads it can learn what his duty is to his mother and father, materially and spiritually. Besides, it can be of benefit to those who are too concerned about the transient things of this world and care little about eternal life.

A copy of the published Welsh translation came into the hands of the recusant John Edwards of Plasnewydd, Chirk. He sent it to Thomas Wiliems of Trefriw to have his opinion of the translation. Wiliems appears to have been dissatisfied, and in a letter to Edwards (NLW 356I) he lists forty-five improvements to the translation, which he termed *variae lectiones*. Until 1992, this letter was the only evidence for the existence of the printed work, but it is now known that one copy has survived and is preserved in the Bibliothèque Mazarine, Paris.

Rhosier Smyth also translated LE THÉATRE DU MOND, the work of a Breton renaissance scholar called Pierre Boaistuau. According to the title-page of this French edition, Boaistuau had originally written the work in Latin, *compose en Latin par P Boaystuau . . . puis traduict par luy mesme en Francois.* LE THÉATRE DU MOND, first published in Paris in 1561, was a popular book. It appeared in twenty editions, some from presses in Rouen, Antwerp and even London. The title of the Welsh translation, rendered from the

French, reads as follows: THEATER DU MOND SEF IW
GORSEDD Y BYD LLE I GELLIR GVVELED TRUENI A LESCNI
DYN O RAN Y CORPH AI ODIDAVVGRVVYDD O RAN YR
ENAID, A SCRIFENVVYD GYNT YN Y PHRANGAEG AG A
GYFIAETHVVYD I'R GYMRAEG DRVVY LAFYR ROSIER SMYTH
O DREF LANELVVY ATHRAVV O THEOLOGYDDIAETH . . . A
BREINTIVVYD YN NINAS PARIS 1615.

There are further orthographical variations in this
publication. As the title-page illustrates, Smyth uses
dd and *ll*, and there are traces of the influence of the
orthography adopted by William Salesbury in such
words as *ei* (his) and in the plural ending -*ae, pethae,
pabae*. He may, of course, have opted for a different
press. Indeed it is even suggested that the imprint is
false and that the book was probably printed in
London. He continued to follow Gruffydd Robert's
rules on borrowings from Latin, such as *ambyddiad* <
ambitio, coined many a Welsh word, like *cynildeb,
barbariaeth*, and used some English derivatives, as in
ffamiliar, caracterau.

The book is a treatise on human life and its wretch-
edness, particularly man's sufferings and God's
retributions; on man's excellence being God's creation and gifted with a soul; on redemption; and on
the godliness in man and the making of his great-
ness. The thesis is authenticated throughout by
quotations from the Church Fathers and classical
works.

One cannot doubt Rhosier Smyth's loyalty and
devotion to his country, to the Catholic Church and
to renaissance thinking. In the preface, dated *Dinas
Paris, 20 o fis Rhagfyr, 1615*, he pleads to possible
critics of his Welsh for sympathetic understanding,

explaining that he had been absent from his country for forty years and adding that he had translated the book to demonstrate his love for Wales in the hope that he could get the Welsh gentry to love their country and be custodians of their language, and the learned to write works for the benefit of Wales.

II

Not all zealous Catholic writers were as interested in the influence of the Renaissance on language and style as Gruffydd Robert, Morys Clynnog and Rhosier Smyth. William Allen, formerly principal of St Mary's Hall, Oxford, founded the Douai seminary for refugee students with the aim of:

The spiritual regeneration of their country, which they believed could only be brought about by the re-establishing of the Holy, Catholic and Roman Church on British soil.

This seminary was established in 1568 in Douai, Brabant, a Spanish territory under the yoke of Philip of Spain. About this time the Dutch prince, William of Orange, invaded and occupied the territory, but soon had to retreat and live in exile, where he was murdered in 1584. One finds a reference to his murder in a poem 'Cowydd Marwnad yn llawn cabledd ar Prins Orens' attributed to a 'Mr White' (Cardiff MS 23, 255–57), which opens with the lines:

> *Tydi Orens tew daeredd,*
> *Da gan bawb dy gau mewn bedd,*

where the author rejoices in his murder. He states that William of Orange had now quitted the Lowlands for the lowest country of all (*o'r wlad isaf . . . i'r is i gyd . . . lle mae vffern* [hell]), where he assures the reader that Luther, Ridley, Jewel and William Salesbury, *y translatiwr*, now dwell.

During these political uncertainties the college was moved to Reims in 1578, returning to Douai in 1593. While at Douai between 1570 and 1578 it was attended by twelve students from Wales and the Welsh borders, including the writer Robert Gwyn of Penyberth and Rhosier Smyth, and during the stay at Reims by twenty-seven Welsh students, including William Davies, the poet and martyr. The seminary returned to Douai in 1593 and its registers during the years 1593–1692 contain the names of some forty-four Welshmen.

The founders of the other refugee seminaries had similar exclusively Counter-Reformation aims. A seminary was founded in Valladolid in 1589 and from its foundation till 1670 was attended by thirty-six students from Wales, including John Salisbury of Rug, Merioneth, John Leander Jones of Breconshire, John Roberts of Trawsfynydd, and the author and poet Gwilym Pugh and two of his brothers, Richard and Charles, the grandsons of the recusant Robert Pugh of Penrhyn Creuddyn. King Philip II of Spain visited the Valladolid seminary in August 1591. Speeches of salutation were made by the students in their chosen languages. John Bennet from the diocese of St Asaph, the senior student, delivered his in Welsh. In it he explained:

That the welshe or british language that was used in Ingland before the entraunce of the Saxons is accoumpted so auncient among us as manie in Ingland do thynke it canne neither be written nor printed. which not onelie reason but experience also of our daies doth manifestlie refute, for that a Catholique Preest and Doctor in diuinitie of that nation hath both writen and printed not long ago a gramer and Cathechisme in the same language on this syde of the seas, and here be diuers in this College that do both speake and write the same verie well, and do hope to preache therein also one daie, to their countrie men when their lotte comme to returne home. (As printed in La ENSENANZA DEL INGLÉS EN ESPANA, S. Martin-Gamero, Madrid, 1961.)

A preparatory school for the sons of recusants was opened by Robert Persons at St Omer in 1593. It was forced to change its location from time to time to such cities as Liège, Ghent and Watten. Twelve names of pupils from Wales appear on the registers from the day of opening till 1691.

The timetable for each day at these seminaries was very strict and intense, with long hours of devotions from six o'clock in the morning, followed by lessons and private studies with sessions for services, confession and contemplation. Latin and Greek were taught, and within the course of three years all students had to read the Old Testament twelve times and the New Testament sixteen times, using the Vulgate, and to study the works of the Christian Fathers. They also followed specific courses in religious controversy and in the art of preaching as part of their training as missionary priests to serve in their homeland. One Douai student, Martin Gregory, wrote in 1578:

We preach in English in order to acquire greater power and grace in the use of the vulgar tongue, and by which the heretics plume themselves exceedingly and by which they do injury to the simple folk.

The recusant lists of the Elizabethan reign in no way provide a true guide to papal loyalty in Wales. Between the years 1559 and 1603 the number of registered recusants in each Welsh diocese was as follows: Bangor 34, St Asaph 250, St David's 145 and Llandaff 361. During the same period, the Welsh language had displaced Latin as the language of public worship in the Welsh parish churches. The Anglican Prayer Book and the New Testament had been translated into Welsh in 1567. And with the failure of the Spanish Armada in 1588 and the publication of William Morgan's translation of the whole Bible, which was supplied to all churches, the Catholic missionary priests in Wales by the end of the reign were faced with a formidable task.

Although it was unlawful to give shelter to mission-ary priests, a number of families were brave enough to do so. They included homes and locations like Penrhyn Creuddyn, Llwyndyrus and Plas Du in the diocese of Bangor, Erbistock and Plasnewydd, Chirk in the diocese of St Asaph, and Grosmont, Kemeys, Machen, Van near Caerphilly, Llanharan and St Donat's in the diocese of Llandaff. Some noblemen befriended recusants and Catholic priests and writers, such as Maurice Wynn of Gwydir, Sir John Salesbury of Lleweni, Edward Somerset of Raglan, the Turbervilles of Pen-llin in the Vale of Glamorgan, Edward and John Gam of Drenewydd, Brecon, Morgan Meredydd of Bugeildy, Radnor, William Hanmer of Fenns Hall, Maelor Saesneg, and John ap Huw ap Madog of Plas Pickhill, Bangor Is-coed.

The Act of Uniformity of 1559 had prohibited writing, printing, teaching and preaching anything in defence of the papal authority, spiritual or ecclesi-astical. Anybody who did so would be *subject to the following penalties, £20, one year's imprisonment . . . for the second offence, the penalties of praemunire, the third offence to be deemed high treason.* The English refugees, in order to circumvent these prohibitions, embarked in 1563 on a policy of publishing English books abroad and sending them secretly to England. In 1575 some licensed London presses had begun to publish Catholic books secretly, and by 1580 secret presses had been set up in England which printed books, often concealing the identity of authors, without imprints or with false imprints, undated or pre-dated. There is definite evidence that one secret press was active in Wales in 1586–7. Eighteen of these unlicensed English presses are known to have printed at least fifty-three recusant books. Hundreds of English books were printed abroad, most of them with genuine imprints, others ascribed to fictitious printers.

It was the recognized policy of William Allen as head of the Douai Seminary to publish English Catholic books. In the opinion of Jean Vendeville, regius professor of canon law at Douai, writing in 1580, this policy was apparently deemed a success in England:

To bring about the change of mind certain books of our men in English concerning almost all matters of controversy, formerly made and printed in Flanders, had done much; in which, for the comprehension of the people, with a wonderful clarity almost all the deceits of the heretics and their consequences, their disputes, blasphemies, contradictions, absurdities, falsifying both of the Scriptures and Doctors of the Church were exposed; so that in every matter not only in the judgement of the wise but also of the people we were superior, nor at any point were our adversaries equal to us save only in the power of their prince and in arms and in the orders of the laws.

The attitude of the Douai writers towards language as a medium of communication differed completely from that of their Welsh counterparts in Rome. At no time did they teach as the Renaissance linguists did that literature in the vulgar tongue should imitate the classical style. A. C. Southern, the authority on English recusant prose, states:

Primarily, as must be evident, they were not concerned with literature as an accomplishment at all. Their business was to combat what they believed to be error and to expose the truth, not to produce literary masterpieces, and their writing is altogether directed towards this end . . . It is clear that they aimed at a simple straightforward exposition of their themes, such as would appeal to the unlearned.

The author Richard Shacklock also explains why he used spoken English in his book THE HACHET OF HERESYES (1565):

No man is so wel inbued with the knowledge of forren tonges, but when a matter of greate importance is tolde hym, the truthe of which he is desyrouse to knowe certaynly, and to which he is mynded to make an aunswer wysely, had rather haue it declared in his natyral and mother tonge be it neuer so barbarouse, then in a straunge language be it neuer so eloquent.

The first few books published by Douai writers were:

AN ANSWERE TO MASTER JUELLES CHALENGE, Thomas Harding (Louvain, 1564)
A CONFUTATION OF A BOOKE INTITLED AN APOLOGIE OF THE CHURCH OF ENGLAND, Thomas Harding (Antwerpe, 1565)
A PROUFE OF CERTEYNE ARTICLES OF RELIGION DENIED BY M JUELL, Thomas Dorman (Antwerpe, 1564)
A CONFUTATION OF A SERMON, John Rastell (Antwerpe, 1564)

DEFENSE AND DECLARATION OF THE CATHOLICKE DOCTRINE, William Allen (Antwerpe, 1565).

These books were written to refute the criticism of Catholic dogma by John Jewel, bishop of Salisbury. He had declared in a sermon delivered at St Paul's Cross, London, in 1559:

If any learned man of all our adversaries or if all the learned men that be alive be able to bring any one sufficient sentence out of any old catholic doctor or father or out of any old general council, or out of the holy scriptures of God or any one example of the primitive church, whereby it may be clearly & plainly proved that there was any private mass in the whole world at that time for the space of six hundred years after Christ, or that there was then any communion ministered unto the people under one kind, or that the people had their common prayer then in a strange tongue that they understood not, or that the bishop of Rome was then called an universal bishop, or the head of the universal church, or that the people was then taught to believe that Christ's body is really, substantially, corporally, carnally or naturally in the sacrament . . . If any man were able to prove any of these articles, I would give over and subscribe to it.

The sermon was published in both Latin and English in 1562, bearing the titles APOLOGIA ECCLESIAE ANGLICANAE and AN APOLOGIE OF THE CHURCH OF ENGLAND.

One of the Welsh students at Douai who had actually heard John Jewel delivering this sermon at St Paul's Cross was Robert Gwyn. He writes: *Onyd oyddwn a'm llygaid yn gwrando?* ('Did I not witness it?'). His name appears on the college register in 1571 as *Robertus Guinus, Bangorensis . . . ex antiquorum Britonum natione.* Unlike the previous writers whose works we have mentioned, a certain amount is known about Robert Gwyn. He was the son of John Wyn ap Thomas Gruffydd of Penyberth near Pwllheli and had been brought up a Protestant. After graduating in Humanities at Corpus Christi, Oxford, in 1568, he decided to embrace the Catholic faith and join his relative, Robert Owen of Plas Du, as a student in Douai. After completing the three-year seminary course he followed a B.D. degree course at Douai University, qualified in 1575 and was ordained priest. His tutor at the seminary was Thomas Stapleton, a Latin scholar known especially for his translation into English of Bede's HISTORIA ECCLESIASTICA GENTIS ANGLORUM, published in 1565 as A FORTRESS OF THE FAITH.

We have previously referred to the custom of letter-writing, which was promoted among students by William Allen. Robert Gwyn, like other students, took to the habit of writing such letters to his family during his stay at the seminary. GWYRTHIAU'R GWŶR NEWYDD, the first, so he states, was on the subject of miracles that the reformers (*novationes*) claimed to perform, and the second was entitled FOD EGLWYS GRIST YN UN CORFF (*Christ's Church is one body*). Both these letters are lost, but his third, a lengthy treatise, bearing the title of THERE CAN BE NO OTHER FAITH OTHER THAN THE TRUE FAITH (*Na all fod Vn ffydd onyd y wir Ffydd*), has been preserved in a composite manuscript called LANTER GRISTNOGAWL (*Christian Lantern*) (pp. 62–220), written in August 1604 by a professional scribe called William Dafydd Llywelyn of Llangynidr in the Usk Valley, Breconshire. Robert Gwyn's name appears on its frontispiece, and he is described by the scribe as 'one of the most cultured persons from Rome to St David's, Menevia' (*vn o gwyr gore o ddysg ag oedd o Ryfain i du ddewi myniw*).

His letter is really an attempt to answer John Jewel's challenge. He actually refers to Jewel's sermon:

Yn gimiint a ffregethy o esgobyn ffalst o salsbri yn eglwys bowls yn llynden . . . ger bron stat y dernas od oedd vn nag arall or hen ffordd alle ddangos vn Rheswm, vn gair ne vn tittyl mewn llyfyr nag ysgrifen o fiawn y 6, c kyntaf o flynyddoedd ar ol crist. Os galle vn or hen ffordd ddangos yddo vn gair o vn or doctoried or amser hwnw, ef yn gwic addefe y fod ef dros y ffordd ag y fydde or hen ffydd.

(Seeing that the false bishop of Salisbury declared at St Paul's in London . . . in the presence of parliament that if anybody at all of the old way could give any reason, one word or title in a book or writing belonging to the first six hundred years AD; if anyone of the old way could point out to him any single word from the works of the doctors from that period, he would quickly confess that he had gone astray and would conform with the old faith.)

He also comments on the success of the Douai writers in refuting John Jewel's challenge, stating that 'they had proved all the points with the aid of the works of the Christian Fathers that had been written during the first six centuries' (*Hwy a ai pryfiasson yn glir yr holl byngkie allan or doctoried . . . ar ysgrifenoedd o fewn cwmpas y 6c, mlynedd cyntaf*).

In this letter Robert Gwyn makes a ruthless attack on the Protestants, calling them *nouationes*, or new men (*gwŷr newydd*), lutherans (*lutherried*) and bastards (*bastardied*). He describes Latimer, who was martyred during Mary's reign, as a knave (*cnaf*), and John Jewel as the bishop of foolery (*esgob ffwlbri*) and a false bishop (*esgob ffals*), and describes his book, APOLOGIA, as fallacious (*celwyddog*). He equally reviles reformers like Melanchthon and Zwingli.

His letter is a treatise on Christian doctrine, dealing with the creation, the fall and salvation, and seeks to help the reader to recognize the True Faith, *de vera religione*. It can be recognized, he explains, by its continuity, universality, and power to convert people to the Faith and perform miracles. One must have faith that Christ's Body is present in the Mass (*corporaliter*) and respect sacred images (*de sacris imaginibus*) and believe in invocation of saints (*de invocatione Sanctorum*) and pilgrimage (*peregrinatio*).

He quotes extensively from HISTORIA by Thomas Stapleton, and there is textual evidence that he was familiar with the contents of such works as:

Certen godly learned and comfortable conferences betwene the two Reuerende fathers and holye Martyrs of Christe D, Nicolas Rydley late Bysshoppe of London and M. Hughe Latymer Sometyme Bysshoppe of Worcester during the tyme theyr emprysonmentes (MDLVI)
Themata quae Villegagno in suis aduersus Caluinum libris propugnanda suscepit (Paris, 1561)
Ioannis Ivelli Angli Episcopi Saricburiensis vita & more (1573)

He is rather critical of Morys Clynnog's ATHRAVAETH GRISTNOGAVL, opining that a skeleton outline of Christian doctrine scarcely sufficed, for the Welsh people were so distanced from the Faith. He confesses that Clynnog's Welsh is superior to his, but his defective fluency was not going to stop him trying to strengthen the Welsh people's hold on the Faith.

But his orthography bears no resemblance to that of Clynnog's. In fact it is a muddle. The text itself has no examples of late Latin derivatives. His Welsh is very colloquial and is marked with English words, phrases and syntax. Like that of his mentor Thomas Stapleton in HISTORIA, his style is characterized by the frequent use of what is called 'doubling the expression', for example *nerth a phwer*, a feature commonly found in the English Catholic homiletic writings of the period and advocated by his Douai tutors. The letter was, undoubtedly, intended to be read aloud to members of his family and relatives, for he frequently calls the attention of listeners with such appealing remarks as *gwelwch* or *merkiwch*. He also introduces tales about people bearing identical names to those of members of his family – his father, Siôn Wyn, and both his sisters, Marged and Anne.

Robert Gwyn left Douai and returned to Wales in 1576 and is known to have visited Plas Du, Erbistock and Penrhyn Creuddyn, near Llandudno. In 1578 the Pope granted him the right to bless cassocks and consecrate portable altars. If we take him at his word, he visited Rome in 1580, and it was during this stay abroad, so he states, that he wrote another letter to his parents. In it he actually refers to the city by name: *Beth pete wr or wlad yma (sef yw hono Ryfain) yn dwad i gymry* ('What if a man from this country [namely Rome] were to come to Wales'), and he has this description of his circumstances at the time of writing:

Orfu ymi fod heb gysgu hyd ony chlywn gloch haner nos yn ysgrifeny hyn ar frys, heb gael enyd y dydd. Dyw ay gwyr fod y dagre yn Redeg rhyd fyngryddie lawer dydd yn meddwl am danoch, ag yn enwedic y silie ar diwarnodie ychel yn bennaf yn dwad ym meddwl ag yn pryddhay fynghalon pen y gwelwy i y gwsanaeth prydwysaidd yny gwledydd yma ar ddiwarnode ywchel a gweled y bobyl yny glanhay y hynen o ddi wrth y pechode y foliany duw fel y dylen santyddio pob diwarnod ychel.

(I had to be without any sleep until I heard the midnight bell, writing this hastily, without a moment to spare during the day. God knows that the tears flowed down my cheeks many a day thinking of you, and especially on Sundays. On high festivals mainly I have recollections of you and I am heart-broken when I witness the heavenly services in these countries on festivity days and see the people cleansing themselves of their sins in order to praise God and, as they should, keep holy every high festival.)

William Dafydd Llywelyn added a note at the side of the page to explain to whom Robert Gwyn was referring when he said: *yn meddwl am danoch*. It reads *y vam ay Dad ay vrodyr* ('his mother and his father and his brothers'). But whether this reference to Rome is a cover-up to hide the fact that he was still, contrary to the law, active as a missionary in Wales, it is difficult to decide. But the date 1580 ('Md.80') does appear in the text as the date of composition.

The only surviving copy of the letter, known as 'Gwssanaeth y Gwŷr Newydd' is also preserved in the composite manuscript LANTER GRISTNOGAWL (pp. 1–61v) in the hand of William Dafydd Llywelyn. The Council of Trent in 1562 had declared it a sin for Catholics to attend heretical services, and Pope Pius V had confirmed it in 1566. Douai writers quickly published a number of books warning their fellow Catholics at home to refrain from attending Anglican services, as they were by so doing putting their own salvation at risk. The arguments found in Gregory Martin's TREATISE OF SCHISME (1578) and Robert Persons's A BRIEF DISCOURS CONTAYNING CERTAYNE REASONS WHY CATHOLIQUES REFUSE TO GOE TO CHURCH (1580) are repeated in Robert Gwyn's letter.

He explains in his preface that there are amongst his

fellow countrymen two types: those who endanger their souls by innocently attending Anglican services, and those who have been informed that it is a sin to do so but still persist, hoping that they will see better days and that God will show his mercy. This is followed by a discussion of such matters as listening to Church of England services, socializing with schismatics, the conviction that there is no salvation outside the Catholic Church, that martyrdom is to be preferred to the denial of the Faith, the fallacy of attending church but not participating in the service, and church vows. He bases his arguments on quotations from the Vulgate and Christian Fathers. This is followed by an addendum on the dangers of living a worldly life.

He refers to the disappearance of the old Latin Missals (*hen lyfre fferen lladin*), which in 1547, during the reign of Edward VI, were forbidden by statute to be used in Anglican churches, and compares them with the Welsh Book of Common Prayer (1567), *y llyfre kiminwyn newydd*, where there is no mention of the Mass, the invocation of saints and unction. Some of his relatives at home in Llŷn are mentioned, such as Sir John Wyn of Bodfel (*ob.* 1575), former standard-bearer to the earl of Warwick at Norwich in 1549, who was granted the Isle of Bardsey for his services.

Robert Gwyn by the early 1580s thought it wise to distance himself from his family lest his recusancy should endanger them. Like Robert Southwell he had, to adapt Southwell's words:

bridled his desire to see them, with care and jealousy of their safety, and banishing himself from the seat of his cradle in his own country, he had lived like a foreigner, and found among strangers that which in his nearest blood he presumed not to see.

He had found sanctuary at Werngochen near Abergavenny. There in his priest-hole in 1583–4 he wrote a massive 364-page tome called Y DRYCH KRISTNOGAWL (*The Christian Mirror*). Many copies (*aml gopiae*) of this work were made, but only one has survived (Cardiff MS 3.240). This copy, dated 1600, is in the hand of Llywelyn Siôn (1540–1615), a recusant and professional scribe from Llangewydd in the Vale of Glamorgan, whose services as a scribe were much in demand by Welsh Catholic writers following the restrictions on the printing of Catholic works. He was also a poet and master of the traditional Welsh strict metres who was more than ready to eulogize his Catholic writers and patrons, as his poems to Siôn Dafydd Rhys and Tomas Lewys o'r Fan testify.

Robert Gwyn, as we have already mentioned, had pursued a course on religious controversy and the art of preaching at Douai. He was described by a contemporary biographer as *a learned theologian and a most eloquent preacher*. Y DRYCH KRISTNOGAWL, in its content and the fluency of its homiletic style, is ample evidence of this. The book is an exposition of the teaching of the Catholic Church on the Four Last Things: Death, the Day of Judgement, Hell and Heaven, amply evidenced by quotations from the Scriptures, the Christian Fathers of the first six centuries and the works of the schoolman Dionysius Carthusianus (1402–71). The Puritan martyr John Penry, in his attempt to bring the book into disrepute, compares it with the works of Dionysius Carthusianus, Didachus Stella and Robert Persons, the three authors most hated by the Anglican, Lutheran and Calvinistic establishment. In his opinion it was nothing more than a collection of fables and Frier Rush (a typical emissary of the devil).

To Robert Gwyn the simple and familiar spoken language should be used whilst preaching and instructing ordinary folk in the Faith:

In order to enable the simple folk to understand the book and benefit from it, I have set out my thoughts before them in the most common and vulgar tongue in use amongst the Welsh.

He uses the unadulterated colloquial Welsh of his native Eifionydd and Llŷn, but doubles some expressions, frequently pairing up words in common use in the southern counties with his own. His translations from Scripture are far from literal, and he makes no apologies for punctuating his translations from the Christian Fathers with dramatic touches. His orthography bears no resemblance to that of Gruffydd Robert. He appears to be completely ignorant of Robert's recommendations on word formation and unaware of his emphasis on regularity and copiousness of expression. In 1580 a meeting of missionary priests in the home of William Griffith, a native of Llancarfan, was held at Uxbridge in the vicinity of London to discuss the possibility of setting up secret printing presses. Robert Gwyn was present at that meeting. It was decided to set up a secret press in London, later known as Green Street House Press. Five books were printed at this press in 1580–1, three bearing the false pressmark Douai and two the false pressmark Louvain. Other secret presses followed, including one in Wales. As Robert Gwyn was the leader of the secular priests in Wales, we cannot but presume that it was established at his instigation. It was set up in 1586–7 in a coastal cave at Rhiwledyn on land owned by Robert Pugh of Penrhyn in Eglwys Rhos, a border parish between the two dioceses of Bangor and St Asaph.

Robert Pugh had registered as a student at the Middle Temple in 1567, but he does not appear to have followed the profession of lawyer. In 1582 his name appeared on the recusant list for Eglwys Rhos, along with that of his wife, the daughter of Sir Richard Bulkeley of Baron Hill, Beaumaris. He is described by his grandson Gwilym Pugh as a devout Catholic who would not venture anywhere without a priest (*nid âi byth heb offeiriad ac offeren*).

In 1586 Herbert, lord of Pembroke and president of the Council of Wales and the Marches, started his campaign against recusants. Robert Pugh was suspected of giving shelter to Catholic priests and was reported to have set up a press on his land. Robert Pugh, William Davies, who had newly re-turned as a missionary priest from Reims, and, according to John Penry, a printer named Roger Thackwell were involved in the printing. This illegal activity was discovered by the agents of the local justice of the peace, Sir Thomas Mostyn of Glodd-aith, but all of those implicated were allowed to escape. Robert Pugh fled to Lancaster and sought refuge with the Houghton family of Lea Hall, Preston. Additionally a letter to the archbishop of Canterbury written by Dr William Griffith, justice of the peace for Caernarfon, mentions that a press was active in the cave in 1587. John Penry refers to a book *written in Weltch, printed in an obscure cauie in North-wales published by an author vnknown* in the same year, and Gwilym Pugh says that the book printed was DRÛCH CRISTNOGAWL, adding that it was printed *ar gwascbren . . . o fewn y bryn* ('on a hand press constructed of wood inside the hill').

Only the first section of the manuscript was printed, *Y Drych Cyntaf* ('The First Mirror'), which deals with:

The necessity of thinking about spiritual matters.
The obligation to love God above all for it is he who created us.
By his act of salvation God revealed his love for man.
The Heavenly Kingdom.

The text and preface are falsely attributed to well-known refugee writers. The text is signed: *O FYLAN, yr eiddoch G.R.*, and the preface: *O DREF ROAN, eich gwladwr caredig, R.S.* The title-page bears the obviously false Rouen imprint, *Rhotomagi apud haeredes Iathroi Fauonis*, and the date *1585* is an example of pre-dating. The literary style of *Y Drych Cyntaf* is so different from that of Gruffydd Robert and so similar to that of Robert Gwyn that one must conclude that G.R. is R.G. inverted and stands for Robert Gwyn, and that R.S. stands for Robert Siôn, Robert Gwyn's alias, the son of John Wyn. Robert Gwyn used the alias Robert Johns Gwyn in another of his works, as we shall see.

On the final page is printed *Gweddi S.T.M.*, a translation of Sir Thomas More's Prayer. Thomas More (1478–1535), the lord chancellor, had argued against making the king Head of the Church. He was brought to trial and a verdict of guilty was procured. In 1535 he was executed and his head fixed on London Bridge. This prayer was frequently printed by Catholic authors, including Thomas Stapleton, in their devotional books that were printed abroad at the time.

Two copies of another of Robert Gwyn's works, COELIO'R SAINT (*Believing the Saints*) have survived in manuscripts Cardiff MS 2.82 and Havod MS 6, both in the hand of Llywelyn Siôn. In the last-mentioned copy, which is attributed to *Robert Johns Gwyn*, we find an obvious attempt to imitate the orthography of Gruffydd Robert. The text is arranged in what the author calls *llithiau* (readings). The style is homiletic, and the frequent use of word-forms from south Wales denotes that this copy was intended to be read in homes in the southern counties. Robert Gwyn maligns the Protestants (*y gwŷr newydd*), calling them *hereticiaid* (heretics), *gelynion yr aberth* (enemies of the Mass), *gau weision eglwysig* (the false servants of the church), *Kalvin a'i hiliogaeth* (Calvin and his progeny), *kalvin gelwyddog, eu meistr pennaf hwy dan Satan* (the false Calvin, their supreme leader under Satan).

This work is a further attack on John Jewel, and it may have been occasioned by the appearance of Maurice Kyffin's Welsh translation of Jewel's APOLOGIA, DEFFYNNIAD FFYDD EGLWYS LOEGR, which was published in London in 1595. In his preface Kyffin explains that he was seeking to reveal the 'impurity of the belief of the Pope of Rome' (*amhuredd crediniaeth Pab Rhufain*), and Robert Gwyn in reply deals with the relevant canons of faith in twelve chapters, over 300 pages, defending as usual with quotations from Scripture and the Christian Fathers. The canons are the presence of Christ at the Mass, communion by bread alone, praying for the dead, invocation of saints, pilgrimages and images.

Lesser-known writers such as Rowland Puleston, the author of LLEFR O'R CHRISTNOGEDD, which remains in a manuscript written in 1582–3 (NLW MS 7163), similarly ridicules papists who follow the fantasies of the Roman Anti-Christ (*y papists, y pabeddolwyr . . . y rhain sy yn calyn dychmygion y Rhufenol Antichrist*), and such devotions as the prayer for the dead, fasting, crosses, purgatory, images, the use of Latin in services, unction and monasticism. He praises the martyrs who suffered under the cruel Queen Mary (*y creulon frenhines Mari*), but describes Elizabeth as the gracious queen (*y grasol frenhines Elizabeth*).

So far we have dealt with Robert Gwyn's original works. His contribution to new recusant writings is quite prolific, and the volume of his creative works secures him a high place amongst Elizabethan Welsh authors. But he was also a translator. We can safely attribute to Robert Gwyn the part-translation and adaptation of the Latin work of the Spanish author Francisco Toledo, SUMMA CASUUM [*sic*] CONSCIENTIAE SIVE DE INSTRUCTIONE SACERDOTUM, a treatise on moral theology. One copy has survived, Havod 14, a manuscript of 126 pages. Toledo was a tutor at the University of Rome before he was appointed cardinal in 1594. The treatise was translated into Spanish in 1616 and French in 1628. The original Latin text circulated in manuscript form throughout Europe before it was printed in 1599, and was highly recommended as a manual for confessors. Toledo declares his indebtedness to Martin Aspilcueta or Dr Navarus, the author of MANUAL DE CONFESSORES (1557). Robert Gwyn chooses, translates or paraphrases those sections that he thinks relevant to the Welsh situation.

The opening sections of the Latin original deal extensively with confession to priests. As there was a scarcity of priests in Wales, he skips over these sections, concentrating on Christian charity, uncharitableness, the ill-treatment of servants, fasting, witchcraft, sins against the Catholic faith, the Ten Commandments, adultery, divorce, incest, rape, sodomy, theft, the repayment of debts, usury, the commandments of the Church, keeping the Sabbath, listening to Mass, fasting, marriage and confession.

The marks of ownership on the manuscript testify that it had been handled by relatives and friends of Robert Gwyn. John Wyn was a popular family name, and Henry Evans, Penrhos, was a close neighbour. Some of the named were known recusants and sympathizers like John Griffith, Cefnamwlch in Llŷn and Thomas Madrun of Cefn Madryn. The reference to the sin of piracy and to John Wyn of Bodwrda, the well-known captain of the pirates of Enlli, and to the custom of herring fishing, two things not mentioned in the original Latin, definitely link this translation with Robert Gwyn, as does his customary homiletic style of writing.

Robert Gwyn also translated a popular English book of devotion, A MANVALL OR MEDITATION AND MOST NECESSARY PRAYERS WITH A MEMORIAL OF INSTRUCTIONS RIGHT REQUISITE. ALSO A SUMMARY OF CATHOLIC RELIGION, which had been printed on a secret press three times between 1580 and 1592. Two copies of the translation in the hand of Robert Gwyn's favourite scribe, William Dafydd Llywelyn, have survived (Llanstephan MS 13 and Swansea Public Library MS A 1.57). The title of the Welsh translation is MEDITASSION. Although Robert Gwyn was of course familiar with *myfyrdod*, the Welsh for meditation, he opted for an English word. Indeed, this translation is dappled with English derivatives, such as *obedient*, *holswm* (wholesome), *ffrinsip* (friendship) and *vertiw* (virtue). Otherwise the Welsh is faultless. Having lived at Werngochen, Abergavenny and served the recusants and patrons of priests in border parishes that were in the gradual process of anglicization, such as Skenfrith, Grosmont, Llandeilo Bertholau, Llangatwg, Llanllowell and Llyswyrny, Robert Gwyn had felt obliged to be more liberal with his use of English words than in the past. English devotional books were scarce, but even if they had been readily available, Robert Gwyn, who travelled much of that country *to reconcile the people to the Romish Religion*, knew of devout families who would prefer to have a Welsh manual of prayers, even if only in manuscript form – and he was prepared to deliver.

How determined the missionary priests were in their effort to restore the Catholic faith and how relentless the authorities in hindering them is evidenced by the martyrdom of the poets Richard White in 1584 and William Davies in 1593. Richard White, of a Protestant Llanidloes family, graduated at Oxford and was employed as a teacher in schools in Maelor, where he was converted to Catholicism by missionary priests. His recusancy drew the attention of the authorities. He was brought before the courts, imprisoned and hanged in Wrexham: *His head and one of his quarters were set up upon Denbigh Castle, and the other three quarters were disposed to Wrexham, Ruthin and Holt.*

Gruffydd Robert had advocated the use of carol metres (*messur carol*) to spread the Faith, and Richard White had taken his advice. Five carols are attributed to White. One of them, which deals with the Four Last Things, was composed whilst he was enduring his three years' imprisonment, as this verse shows:

> *Os bydd gofyn pwy ai kant,*
> *athro plant o Gymro*
> *sydd yn kymryt karchar beth*
> *yn byw mewn gobeth etto.*

(If one asks who composed this, a Welsh teacher of children who is serving his time in prison, still living in hope.)

The metre he used is the *awdl-gywydd*. The content deals with the importance of personal devotions and loyalty to the one and only true Church and its teaching, which the Lutherans deny:

> *Maen hw yn gwadv yr ysgrythvr lan*
> *gida i man gelwdde,*
> *ar dogtorieid gidar saint*
> *oedd vawr i braint ai gwrthie.*

(They are denying the Holy Scriptures with their little lies whilst the doctors and the saints were highly privileged with their miracles.)

One carol is a paraphrase of one of Robert Persons's early publications, A Brief Discours contayning certayne Reasons why Catholiques refuse to goe to Church (Doway, 1580). In it he attacks those who deny the Mass, who burn images and who disrespect the saints and feast days.

According to the Bodley Library copy of the Welsh bibliography, Cofrestr o'r Holl Lyfrau Cofrestredig, compiled by Moses Williams, the carols were printed in 1600 without an imprint. David Rogers's comment reads:

Accepting that White's Carolau was printed in 1600, the safest guess would be that it was printed secretly somewhere in Wales, or possibly by some press established near its border. The absence of an imprint makes a secret press at home slightly more probable than a press overseas.

We have referred to William Davies previously as a student at Reims and as one of the persons who assisted with the printing of Y DRYCH CHRISTIAN-OGAWl in the Rhiwledyn cave. He was arrested in 1592 after serving on the mission in north Wales for seven years, brought to trial, imprisoned and hanged in Beaumaris in 1593 – *tractus, suspensus, extenteratus, et in partes dissectus, Beaumaritii in Insula Mona.* In Gwilym Pugh of Penrhyn's opinion, he had earned the worthy title of *Syr William, seren ei wlad* ('Sir William, star of his country'). He was born in Croesyneirias of a family known for their cultural interests. His grandfather was Dafydd Nantglyn, who was licensed as a harpist at the Caerwys Eisteddfod in 1523. William Davies may have composed numerous carols of a religious kind, but only one has come down to us, namely *Karol Santaidd i'r Grawys* ('A Holy Carol for Lent'). He used a similar metre – *awdl-gywydd* – to that used by Richard White.

Two copies of the carol have been preserved in two manuscripts (Peniarth 254 and Cwrtmawr 203) copied around about 1609 by John Jones of Gellilyfdy while he was serving in Ludlow as an attorney at the Council of Wales and the Marches. There is no knowing whether John Jones had

Catholic sympathies. If not, his sectarian loyalty did not restrain him from preserving this carol, which is very Catholic in its tone – an appeal for Catholics to be loyal to the Catholic Church, to reject Protestantism (*gwrthod ffordd y pechod mawr*), and to keep the feast of Lent by fasting and self-denial in the Catholic way:

> *Ond byw yn lân y grawys glân*
> *yn yr eglwys lân gatholic*
> *gwrthod ffordd y pechod mawr,*
> *sydd yma yn awr sethredig.*

But the poet himself does refer to his own persecution and to his imprisonment, to the time he spent in the Rhiwledyn cave, or, it may be, to his seclusion in some 'priest-hole' (*yn gaeth mewn kongyl*), where, he says, he composed the carol:

> *O daw govyn pwy ai gwnaeth,*
> *dyn sydd gaeth mewn kongyl.*
> *Rhac y bobyl vawr i chwant*
> *syn gyrrv kant ir kythrel.*

(If anyone asks who composed it, it is a man confined to a corner to avoid insolent people who drive hundreds to the devil.)

The prohibition of printing facilities created a constant demand for the services of the professional scribes, Catholic and non-Catholic, not only to reproduce new recusant writings but also to disseminate Catholic writings of pre-Elizabethan days.

William Dafydd Llywelyn made a copy of a translation executed by Arthur ap Huw, a Marian priest at Tywyn, Merioneth, entitled: BYR DRAETHAWD

AR DRAETHODYL, LLE DANGOSIR PLE DECHREAWYD GYNTA ABERTHU AC OFFRYMMAU AG AM ALLORAU AG EGLWYSEY. AC VAL Y DECHREAWDD FFYDD GRIST GYNTA YN LLOYGER Y MYSCE YR EINGLIS NER SAYSON, WEDY Y WNEYTHUR YN SAESNEG DRWY GORGE MARSHAL YN AMSER MARI VRENHINES . . . DRWY SR A AP H ER CARIAD IR VN FRENHINES AC ER GOLEUO'R PETH YR KYMRO NA WYR SAESNEG. The title of the original English publication reads: A COMPENDIOUS TREATISE IN METRE DECLARING THE FIRST ORIGINALL OF SACRIFICE AND OF THE BUILDING OF AULTURES AND CHURCHES AND OF THE FIRSTE RECEAVINGE OF THE CHRISTEN FAYTH IN ENGLAND . . . G. M. (1555). The poem, the work of the English poet George Marshall (*fl*. 1554), is an onslaught on the Protestant Reformers, making special mention of Wyclif and Luther. Only the first page of the Welsh manuscript has been preserved, just enough for us to have some idea of the metrical form adopted by the translator. He regrets that he does not use the strict metres, but he appeals to the reader not to ignore the message for that reason:

> *na edrychwch ddim am hoffedd*
> *rhif na mesur a chynghanedd*
> *ond ystyriwch drwy hir blesser*
> *ar ddaioni hin o vatter*
> *ac er nad wyfe athryliaithys*
> *nac ychwaith yn gylfeddodys,*
> *na ddiystyrwch ddim or matter*
> *ond pardynwch chwi fy hyder.*

(Do not seek the pleasure of metrical form and cynghanedd, *but pay heed, much to your delight, to the goodness of this content, and although I am neither talented nor artistic, do not disregard any of the content but do excuse my daring.)*

Maurice Kyffin in his preface to DEFFYNNIAD FFYDD EGLWYS LOEGR condemns the custom of publishing the lives of the saints taken from the book of 'monkish lies' called LEGENDA AUREA (*yr hwn a elwid Legenda aurea*). Roger Morris of Coedytalwrn, Llanfair Dyffryn Clwyd (*fl.* 1590), who made frequent use of the orthography of Gruffydd Robert, made copies of translations of medieval texts such as Hugh Pennant's translation of LEGENDA AUREA by the thirteenth-century author Jacobus de Voragine, first printed in Antwerp in 1574 (Llanstephan MS 34), SACRA HISTORIA by Sulpicius Severus (*O gyssegr lân historia Severus Sulpicius*) (NLW MS 1553), which appeared in print for the first time in 1556, and of Severus's LIFE OF ST MARTIN (*Buchedd Martin Sant*). Roger Morris in his preamble gives the history of the translation, attributing it to John Trefor of Trefalun:

John Trevor a droes y vuchedd honn or llading yn Gymraec a Guttun Owain ai hysgrivennodd pan oedd oed krist 1488 yn amser Harri 7, nid amgen y 3 blwyddyn o goronedigaeth yr vn Harri, ac wrth gopi yr vn Guttun yr ysgrivenwyd hwnn. Anno Dni 1582 et 25 Regis Elizabethae.

(John Trevor translated the Life from Latin into Welsh and Guttun Owain transcribed it when Christ's age was 1488 in the time of Henry VII, that is in the third year of the reign of the same Henry, and it was from Guttun's transcript that this copy was made. AD 1582 and the twenty-fifth year of the reign of Elizabeth.

There seems to have been a greater demand for tales about saints in Wales than in England at the time. The earliest English recusant book on the lives of saints appeared in 1609. It was a translation from Italian of FLOS SANCTORUM, a book originally written in Spanish by Alfonso de Villegas.

Roger Morris also made a copy of DRYCH YR UFUDD-DAWD A DYNWYD O LYFREU INNOCENTIWS BAB (Llanstephan 34), which is described as a collection of portions translated from Pope Innocent III's book DE CONTEMPTU MUNDI SIUE DE MISERIA CONDITIONIS HUMANAE.

It appears from the number of surviving copies that the manuscripts copied by Catholic scribes that were in greatest demand were copies of Y BIBYL YNGHYM-RAEG, a translation of PROMPTUARIUM BIBLIAE by Petrus Pictaviensis (Peter of Poitiers), a Paris theologian (*ob.* 1205). It was also translated into German, English and French. Copies of the Welsh translation were made by William Dafydd Llywelyn, Llywelyn Siôn, Siôn Dafydd Rhys and Thomas Wiliems of Trefriw, who completed his copy in 1594, entitling it LLYMA Y BIBL YN YSGRIUENNEDIC YN GYMRAEG, SEF Y PETHAU HISTORI-AWL O'R HEN TESTAMENT YN GRYNNO (BM MS 31055), and who cites from the text in his DICTIONARIUM. Siôn Dafydd Rhys explains that he had made his copy (Llanstephan MS 55) in 1579.

A number of manuscripts copied by Llywelyn Siôn of Llangewydd prove that there was a great demand for copies of earlier pre-Reformation religious trans-lations in Glamorgan and Gwent. The work known by its Latin title DIVES ET PAUPER was originally written in English in 1405 by a Franciscan friar and first published in London in 1493. The Welsh trans-lation explains that the work takes the form of a discussion on the Ten Commandments between a rich man and a poor man:

Yma y diwedda yr ymddiddan a vu rhwng Dives a Phauper, sef yw hynny y tylawd ar kyvoethog, yn traethu or deg gorchymyn yr hwnn lyfr a scryfennwyd y pumed dydd o vis Gorffennaf pan oedd oed Crist 1493 ag a brintwyd gan Risiart pinsen ymyl barr y deml yn llundain.

(Here ends the discourse that happened between Dives and Pauper, that is the poor man and the rich man discussing the Ten Commandments which book was written on the fifth day of the month of July AD 1483 and was printed by Richard Pynson near Temple Bar in London.)

The title of the Welsh translation, which is found in two manuscripts (Cardiff MSS 3.240 [pp.371] and 2.618, an incomplete copy), is DIVES A PHAWPER, and the scribe's name, Llywelyn Siôn, is given:

Ag velly y terfyna y llyfr hwnn am llaw i llen sion o langewydd, y 30 o orffennaf oedran Krist 1600 o dernasad Elizabeth yn grasysaf vrenhines 42.

(Thus ends this book by my hand Llywelyn Siôn of Llangewydd on the 30th of July AD 1600, the forty-second year of Elizabeth's reign, the most gracious queen.)

The fact that he made two copies of the translation at that time means that there was a demand for it, and the number of marks of ownership that appear on the pages is evidence that the manuscripts moved around.

Judging from the character of the Welsh and the frequent use of dialectical forms, the translation is undoubtedly the work of a late medieval Glamorgan author, but it was regarded by Llywelyn Siôn as a suitable work to be re-copied and read in recusant homes at parishes like Tythegston, Newchurch, St Brides, Ewenni and Colwinston.

Another popular book of the period was LE VOYAGE DU CHEVALIER ERRANT, written by Jean de Cartenay, who was born in Valenciennes, France, in 1520. Cartenay attended the Council of Trent and served as adviser to the archbishop of Cambrai during the period when Owen Lewis was canon of Cambrai. He was the author of ten books, the most popular of them LE VOYAGE DU CHEVALIER ERRANT (Antwerp, 1557). During the reign of Elizabeth at least six editions of the original French were published. A German translation, DESS IRRENDEN RITTERS ROISE, appeared in 1602 and a Dutch translation, DE REVSE VAN DEN DOLENDEN RIDDER, in 1649. An English translation was printed ten times between 1581 and 1670. The title of the first was THE VOYAGE OF THE WANDERING KNIGHT. DEUISED BY IOHN CARTHENIE, A FRENCHMAN: AND TRANSLATED OUT OF FRENCH INTO ENGLISH BY WILLIAM GOODYEAR OF SOUTH-HAMPTIN, MERCHANT. A WORK WORTHIE OF READING . . . IMPRINTED AT LONDON . . . 1581. The English translation had been expunged of anything that was distinctly Catholic, and the Welsh translation (Llanstephan MS 178), the work of an unidentified Glamorgan scholar, is almost identical in content to the English version. Several copies of the Welsh translation have survived, the earliest in the hand of the Glamorgan scribe Ieuan ab Ieuan ap Madog, who died in 1587. At least four other copies of the translation have survived, one in the hand of Richard William, a recusant from Battle, near Brecon.

Another Glamorgan scribe who made his contribution to the dissemination of Catholic works was Antoni Powel of Llwydiarth, Llangynwyd, who died in 1618. He transcribed DARN O'R FFESTIVAL (Hafod 22), the work of an unidentified translator. The original English text, LIBER FFESTIALIS, the work of John Mirk, the prior of Lilleshall, Shropshire, is a collection of homilies and was in great demand in the sixteenth century. Another work, known as

GESTA ROMANORUM, a medieval collection of moral tales, was similarly in great demand, and scribes like the recusant Llywelyn Siôn were more than ready to provide copies (Llanofer B 18) for the faithful Catholics of the Vale of Glamorgan.

III

Some of the prime movers of the Welsh Renaissance were refugee Roman Catholics. Whilst abroad, their loyalty to a renewed Roman Church and the hope of its restoration in Wales had become blended with a zeal for Renaissance thought. They hoped for the day when Wales would be restored to Rome and at the same time that Renaissance literary standards and thought would hold sway in Wales. We have already drawn attention to Gruffydd Robert's leading role and the initial contribution of Siôn Dafydd Rhys during his stay in Pistoia. The latter returned to Wales in 1571 a staunch Catholic, having published his third book PERVTILIS EXTERIS NATIONIBUS DE ITALICA PRONVNCIATIONE . . . LIBELLUS two years earlier in memory of Mary, the Catholic queen of England.

After returning, Siôn Dafydd Rhys appears to have been in dire straits for three years. He could scarcely hope to earn his living as a teacher as he had done in Pistoia unless he presented himself as a citizen who willingly accepted Elizabeth as Head of the Church. His Protestant uncle, Richard Davies, the bishop of St David's since 1561, had himself been a refugee on the continent earlier during the reign of Mary and was extremely anti-Catholic, a qualification that led to his appointment as a member of the Council of Wales and the Marches. The bishop appears to have had a strong hold on the returned refugee. In 1574 Siôn Dafydd Rhys was appointed head of Friar's

Grammar School, Bangor, an office that could not be assumed unless he swore the Oath of Supremacy, and two years later he moved to Abergwili at the request of his uncle to assist him with the translation of the Book of Common Prayer and the New Testament, residing in the bishop's palace and following his profession as a qualified physician. His travels as a physician brought him into touch with numerous poets in the vicinity, such as Wiliam Egwad of Llanegwad, Dafydd Llwyd Mathew (*fl.* 1601–29) and Thomas Jones (Twm Siôn Cati, 1530–1609).

When Richard Davies died in 1581 and the new bishop, Marmaduke Middleton, was installed, Siôn Dafydd Rhys was obliged to move out of the palace. He took up residence in Cardiff and continued his practice as a physician. His religious loyalty understandably fluctuated. He befriended Gervase Babington of Llandaff and translated his small catechism into Welsh, discovered a new patron in Sir Edward Stradling of St Donat's and came under the influence of Morgan Clynnog, who had in 1582 established himself as a secular missionary priest in the area.

We have already referred to Siôn Dafydd Rhys's linguistic studies, which were published in northern Italy, and his contribution to the essential task of providing Catholic writings by copying manuscripts. But his *magnum opus* was his grammar of the Welsh language, CAMBROBRYTANNICAE CYMRAECAEVE LINGUAE INSTITUTIONES ET RUDIMENTA (*Rules and Rudiments of the Cambrobritannic or Welsh Language*), which was published by Thomas Orwinus in London in 1592. The cost of printing 1,250 copies was paid by Edward Stradling, to whom the volume is dedicated.

The compilation of the grammar was well in hand as early as 1582. This we gather from a letter Siôn Dafydd Rhys received in that year from William Midleton expressing the hope that part of the grammar would be completed by the time they next met. He may have started on the grammar even before leaving Abergwili. His circuit as a country physician extended to the valleys of the rivers Tywi and Usk and beyond. He states that he had been entertained at the home of Morgan Meredydd at Bugeildy in Radnorshire, and that it was during his frequent visits to this house (*y lle lawer gwaith y bu fawr fy nghroeso a'm hansawdd o fwyd a llyn*) that he compiled the first part of the grammar. He was of the opinion that there was no region in Wales with better people than Breconshire (*nad oedd vn wlad yng Nghymru well ei phobl . . . na phobl wlad Frycheinioc*). This explains why he moved from Cardiff to the town of Brecon in 1583, and it was in a mountain retreat in Clun Hir, Cwm y Llwch, a few miles south of Brecon, that he completed the grammar. He explains this in lines that remind one of Gruffydd Robert's description of the Roman retreat where he had compiled his grammar:

Eithr diweddbarth y Llyfr hynn a fyfyriwyd dan berthi a dail gleision mywn gronyn o fangre i mi fy hunan a elwir y Clun Hir ym mlaen Cwm y Llwch.

(*The latter part of this book was drafted in a small dwelling of mine in a leafy grove known as Clun Hir at the head of the valley of Cwm y Llwch.*)

His intention was to describe the Welsh language not through the medium of Welsh, as Gruffydd Robert had done so excellently, but in Latin, a language known throughout Europe, so that all Europe could get to know about its perfection and magnificence (*perpheithrwydd ac odidawgrwydd*).

The first forty-five pages deal with the pronunciation of Welsh, a subject not touched upon in Gruffydd Robert's grammar. He offers a different solution to some orthographical problems, suggesting, for example, that *d* should be doubled after short vowels, as in *bodd y gwerni* (marsh harrier), but not after a long vowel, as in *cad* (battle). His comments on syntax are limited to the simple sentence and there is no reference to the complex sentence.

A third of the volume (pp. 129–295) deals with *cynghanedd* and the strict metres. Knowing that his treatment is unsafe, he blames the poets whose advice he had sought but who were unready to reveal the secrets of their art, and who were themselves in many cases ignorant of the rules. But when Maurice Kyffin, in his introduction to DEFFYNNIAD FFYDD EGLWYS LOEGR, accused the poets of being ignorant and lacking in learning, Siôn Dafydd Rhys was quick to reply, calling the attack unjust, defamatory and slanderous (*nam a gogan ac enllib*). In defending the poets he blamed the breakdown of traditional patronage. Without the support of the gentry, he argued, the poetic tradition would inevitably decline. He called on the poets to abandon the taverns, befriend the gentry and improve their way of life. They should take a more serious view of their calling and look to the continent for new ideas, so as to become masters anew of their poetic art. He repeated his views in an unpublished document, CYNGOR I FEIRDD A DYSCEDIGION CYMRU (*Advice to the Poets and Learned Men of Wales*) (NLW MS Panton 2).

In 1597 Siôn Dafydd Rhys wrote a treatise (Peniarth MS 118D) criticizing Polydore Vergil's condemnation of Geoffrey of Monmouth's HISTORIA REGUM BRITANNIAE. His criticism of the work of this Renaissance scholar and his own treatises on Welsh traditional history and on the genealogy of King James I tell us more about Siôn Dafydd Rhys's patriotism than about his Renaissance learning. Like his protégé, Gruffydd Robert, he translated a classical text, Aristotle's METAPHYSICS, which unfortunately has not been traced. But there is ample evidence to show that his mastery of his mother tongue had in no way been impaired by his profound interest in other languages, or his stay abroad. Neither did his relationship with prominent members of the Protestant establishment, following his return, distance him from his Catholic past and weaken his deep love for the Catholic faith, as evidenced by his advice to some of his patients to visit St Winifred's Well. He was even accused of setting up a secret press in a house that he rented in the town of Brecon. He was summoned to appear at Ludlow before the Court of Wales and the Marches and in London before the Court of High Commission. But he took the Oath of Allegiance to the Queen and was discharged. Also, to ensure the necessary approval for the printing of his grammar, he took the precaution of adding the following supplication on the final page of the grammar: DOMINE SALUAM FAC REGINAM ('God save the Queen').

We have already mentioned the name of Thomas Wiliems of Trefriw and referred to his recusancy. He was born in 1545 in Ardde'r Mynaich, near Dolgarrog, the son of an illegitimate daughter of Meredydd Wyn of Gwydir. He was educated at Gwydir

School and at Oxford and trained as a physician. He was ordained a deacon to serve in the parish of Trefriw, but left the priesthood to follow his career as a country physician. Throughout his life he was suspected of being a covert Catholic, and he speaks of his harassment by neighbours and of being attacked and robbed of his earnings as he returned from his visits to his patients.

Socially isolated for sectarian reasons, he started to compile a dictionary of the Welsh language, DICTIONARIUM LATINO-CAMBRICUM (Peniarth 228). He gives numerous reasons for undertaking such a task: to do what one could for his country, language and kinsmen, for the preservation of the language, and for its enrichment through borrowings from Latin and from the writings of rhetoricians and philosophers. He lists his sources, which include numerous manuscripts of ancient texts (*hen lyfrau Cymraeg*), which were owned by some of the gentry and which he had been allowed to examine. He names Sir John Wynn of Gwydir, Robert Pugh of Penrhyn, John Edwards of Plasnewydd, Chirk, Huw Gwynn of Berth Ddu, Llanrwst and Edward Thelwall of Plas-y-ward. He makes no mention of Protestant writings, not even the Welsh Bible of William Morgan (1588). He does mention Gruffydd Robert's grammar, Morys Clynnog's catechism and Siôn Dafydd Rhys's grammar, INSTITVTIONES, which was published in 1592. He started writing the final draft of the DICTIONARIUM in May 1604 and completed it in 1607. He followed the format of the Latin–English Dictionary of Thomas Thomas, DICTIONARIUM LINGUAE LATINAE ET ANGLICANIAE, which was published in 1585. He rejects the orthographies of both Gruffydd Robert and Siôn Dafydd Rhys, describing them as inventions for the learned.

Thomas Wiliems's DICTIONARIUM was never printed, but John Davies of Mallwyd used it as the foundation of a part of his dictionary, ANTIQUAE LINGUAE BRITANNICAE DICTIONARIUM DUPLEX, which was printed in 1632.

In a letter written by Thomas Wiliems in September 1615 to his friend John Edwards of Plasnewydd (NLW 3561), he refers to his translation of a booklet, LLYFRAN OR SACRAUEN O BENYT. He was enclosing his translation for Edwards to make a copy. Although it has been lost, this was undoubtedly a translation of A SHORT TREATISE OF THE SACRAMENT OF PENANCE . . . SET FORTH IN ITALIAN BY THE REUEREND FATHER VINCENT BRVNO OF THE SOCIETE OF IESUS, which had been printed in 1605 by the secret press set up by the Jesuit missionary Henry Garnet in England. The title of the original Italian edition was TRATTATO DEL SACRAMENTO DELLA PENITENZA, and it was published in Venice in 1585. Its popularity is evidenced by the fact that it was translated into Latin, Portuguese and French.

Another Catholic writer contemporary with Thomas Wiliems was Richard Vaughan of Bodeiliog, Henllan, Denbigh. He was registered a recusant in 1585 and 1609. He published in 1618 EGLVRHAD HELAETH-LAWN O'R ATHRAWAETH GRISTNOGAWL. A GYFANSODHWYD Y TRO CYNTAF YN ITALAEG, TRWY WAITH YR ARDHERCHOCCAF A'R HYBARCHAF GARDINAL RHOBERT BELLARMIN O GYMDEITHAS YR IESV. AG O'R ITALAEG A GYMREIGWYD ER BUDH YSPRYDOL I'R CYMRU, DRWY DHIWYDRWYDH A DYFAL GYMORTH Y PENBEFIG [sic] CANMOLADWY V.R., PERMISSU SUPERIORUM ('An Ample Explanation of Christian Doctrine composed originally in Italian through the labour of the most venerable Cardinal Roberto Bellarmino of the Society of Jesus, And from Italian translated for the spiritual benefit of the Welsh through the industrious and unfailing assistance of the praiseworthy gentleman V.R.'). Attributing the translation to V.R. successfully concealed his identity. But Gwilym Pugh (1618–1689) made it known later that the translator was not V.R. but R.V., that is Rissiart Vychan (Richard Vaughan). He stated ingeniously:

Chwi ellwch ddarllen yn yr Athrawiaeth Gristnogawl *a wnaeth . . . Cardinal Belarmin o Gymdeithas yr Iessu . . . sudd wedi ei gyfiauthu eir Gymraeg drwy waith Rissiart Vychan o swydd Ddimbech.* (NLW MS 4710)

(*You can read in* Athrawiaeth Gristnogawl *which Cardinal Bellarmino of the Society of Jesus wrote which has been translated into Welsh through the labour of Richard Vaughan of Denbighshire.*)

Most bibliographies in the past attributed the translation to John Salisbury, who was superior of the Welsh Mission of St Francis Xavier at the time of publication. The *Permissu Superiorum* which appears on the title-page probably means that the translation did gain his approval before it was published in St Omer, that is, if the imprint is genuine.

The final sentence in the printed book reads:

Moliant i'r Iesu ag i'w fam fendigedig Mair burforwyn ar Gyfarchiad yr hon y gorphenned hyn o gyfieithiad o'r Italaeg 25 Martii 1618.

(*Praise to Jesus and to his blessed mother, the virgin Mary, on whose Annunciation on the 25 of March 1618 this translation from Italian was completed.*)

Roberto Francesco Romolo Bellarmino, the author of the original Italian text, was born in 1542. He joined the Society of Jesus in 1560, and after serving as professor in the Collegium Romanum he was made cardinal and, later, archbishop of Capua. He published numerous books on Catholic dogma and devotion and assisted with the production of a revised edition of the Vulgate, which appeared in 1591. His catechism appeared in 1598, entitled DICHIARAZIONE PIU COPIOSA DELLA DOTTRINA CRISTIANA, COMPOSTA PAR ORDINE DI N.S. PAPA CLEMENTE VIII, DAL R.P. ROBERTO BELLARMINO. At least five of his works were translated into English, including his catechism AN AMPLE DECLARATION OF THE CHRISIAN [sic] DOCTRINE COMPOSED IN ITALIAN BY THE RENOWMED [sic] CARDINAL. CARD. BELLARMIN, TRANSLATED INTO ENGLISH BY RICHARD HADOCK, Doway, 1604.

As the title of the original Italian text indicates, Bellarmino undertook the work of compiling the catechism by order of Pope Clement VIII. The very year of its publication, Pope Clement declared that no catechism should be published nor used in schools and churches other than Bellarmin's. It was translated into sixty languages, including Arabic.

Undoubtedly, as a translator Richard Vaughan was a novice. His Welsh is not without its defects. For example, he uses the plural form of the verb *bod* (to be) as a copula (*a'r tri pherson hyn ydynt vn vnic Dduw*), the plural form of the verb in affirmative relative clauses (*eneidiau'r Plantos a fuont feirw*), and the third person plural of the verb when the subject of the simple sentence is plural (*Gallant yr Angylion*). He introduces an indirect question with *os* rather than *a* (*cael gwybod os oes*), and uses plural nouns after numerals (*a'r saith Sacrafenneu*). And so on.

His orthography is irregular. Thus plural endings vary between *-au, -eu, -ae* and *-e*, and his mutations are defective, as in *eu anrhydedd nhwy* or *eyn iechydwriaeth*. He appears to follow the directive of Siôn Dafydd Rhys regarding the use of the circumflex, applying it throughout to long vowels in monosyllabic nouns, such as *tîr, chwêch* and *hûn*. His regular use of the possessive form of the personal pronoun *ei* is sufficient evidence that he was familiar with the works of William Salesbury.

Bellarmino's catechism was challenged by Protestants. Rondl Davies, in his PROFIAD YR YSBRYDION NEU DDATCUDDIAD GAU ATHRAWON (1675), a translation of his own A TRYALL OF THE SPIRITS OR A DISCOVERY OF FALSE PROPHETS, specifically mentions Bellarmino as one of the false prophets and condemns Latin services, Mass and the claim that the Pope was the Vicar of Christ. The teaching of the Roman Church was to be avoided by every man who cared for the salvation of his soul (*i'w gochelyd yn ofalus gan bob dyn sydd yn caru jechydwriaeth ei enaid*).

From the turn of the century the Catholic mission had gained strength with the increase of young enthusiastic missionary priests from the various seminaries abroad. In 1605 a residence called Cwm in the parish of Llanrhyddol, situated on the Herefordshire side of the river Monnow, became a hiding place for Richard Griffith, a Jesuit who hailed from the diocese of Bangor and who had been a student at the English College at Valladolid. Another student, John Salisbury from Valladolid, returned to Wales in

1604 and served as resident chaplain at the home of William Morgan and Frances Somerset, the sister of the marquis of Worcester, who had his seat at Raglan Castle. Robert Jones, a native of Chirk and a student at the Seminarium Anglicum in Rome, after a period as lecturer in philosophy at Collegium Romanum, returned to Wales and set up a separate mission for Wales and the border counties, with its headquarters at Cwm. At his death in 1615, John Salisbury became superior of the mission, which in 1621 came to be known as 'the District of St Francis Xavier within the Welsh Mission'. Another major change came about in 1667 when the northern counties of Wales, together with the County of Salop, were grouped together as a separate administration, to be known as the Mission or Residence of Saint Winifred, with its centre at Holywell in Flintshire. John Salisbury died in 1625 and John Clare was appointed superior. He died in 1628 and Charles Browne alias Gwynne, son of Thomas Wyn of Bodfel in Llŷn, who had been educated in Douai, became superior.

In 1647 another Welshman, Humphrey Evans from Caernarfonshire, a former student at Oxford and at the Seminarium Anglicum in Rome, was made superior of the St Xavier Mission, and in 1663 superior of the Mission of St Winifred. Other leading Jesuits were active in Wales. David Lewis, alias Charles Baker of Abergavenny, who was educated at the Seminarium Anglicum, joined the Welsh Mission and was twice made superior. He suffered martyrdom at Usk in 1679. Philip Evans, also educated in Rome, joined the Welsh Mission in 1665. He was seized at the house of Christopher Turberville at Sgêr, imprisoned and executed in Cardiff in 1679. William Morgan was born in Flintshire and was educated at Westminster Grammar School and at the Seminarium Anglicum. After a period as professor of English and Greek at Liège, he was sent on the mission to north Wales. In 1672 he was made superior of the Residence of St Winifred and chaplain in Powys Castle.

During the same period twenty-nine secular priests were active in Wales, the senior amongst them being Morgan Clynnog. Nine Benedictine priests had found patrons at Hawarden Castle (Flintshire), Rotherwas (Herefordshire) and Blackbrook (Gwent). The most notable of these was Gwilym Pugh of Penrhyn.

In 1678, during the Titus Oates Plot, the bishop of Hereford, Dr Herbert Croft, who had for some time been very aware of religious subversion in his diocese, felt that it was necessary to take action. He had been educated in Jesuit colleges at St Omer and Rome, but on returning to his country had abandoned Roman Catholicism and been ordained an Anglican priest. Soon he became dean of Hereford, and bishop in 1661. He sent investigators to the headquarters of the Jesuit Mission at Cwm, Llanrhyddol. In the report, 'A Short Narrative of the discovery of a College of Jesuits at a place called Come in the County of Hereford', which he submitted to the House of Lords in 1679, this information is given:

In one of these houses there was a study found, the door thereof very hardly to be discovered, being placed behind a bed, and plastered over like the wall adjoining, in which was found great store of divinity books, and others in folio and quarto, and many other lesser books, several horse-loads (but they are not yet

brought to me, it being Christmas holy days, but they remain in
safe hand), many whereof are written by the principal learned
Jesuits . . . They are several books written and printed against
the Protestant religion, and many small Popish Catechisms,
printed and tied up in a bundle and some Welsh Popish books
lately printed and some Popish manuscripts fairly and lately
printed.

The most outstanding Welsh figure amongst Welsh
Catholic writers of the seventeenth century was
Hugh Owen of Gwenynog, Llanfflewin, Anglesey.
Hugh Owen was born in 1575. He was self-educated
in law and languages, having learned French,
German, Italian and Dutch. After inheriting the
Gwenynog estate, he started to play a leading role in
the life of the Anglesey gentry. He was made leader
of the local militia, a trained band of 280 soldiers in
the Hundred of Talybolion, and became estate agent
for Sir Huw Owen, Bodeon, one of the leading
members of the shire gentry. He left Anglesey in
1621, and his son John Hughes explains why:

Hugh Owen of Gwenynog . . . a devout Catholique, who for the
profession of the Catholique Faith was constrained to forsake his
Country where he was therefore detained prisoner (vntill he
redeemed his liberty with a merciless bribe) by the Pseudo-Bish.
of Bang, Lewis Bayly, a man, who though by English
Protestants may be esteemed a Sainct because of his seeming
godliness in the book he called The Practise of Piety *(wherein*
whatsoever is good & orthodox was taken out of Cath Authors)
yet is famously knowen in those parts to have lived a lewd
notorious epicure & atheisticall hypocrite. (Stonyhurst MS
A.II)

According to the bishop, writing in 1625, Hugh
Owen had been *a felon. a Romishe recusant who about*
three yeares ago before had given over his place, disposed

of his lands and converted his estate into money, and went out of the countrey, and no man knew why.

He had departed because he feared persecution. He moved to Gwent, found security in the household of the Somersets and was appointed secretary to Henry Somerset, whom he served for twenty years, living for most of the time in Raglan Castle. He retired to Chapel Hill, near Tintern Abbey, where he died in 1642 and where he was buried. In his will he bequeathed *all his books, writings and papers to his son Hugh Owen upon his return.*

The son, Hugh Owen, alias John Hughes, was at that time a student at the Seminarium Anglicum. On his return he found amongst his father's papers three Welsh translations: DE IMITATIONE CHRISTI by Thomas à Kempis; THE BOOK OF RESOLUSION, FROM THE AUTHOR'S LATEST AND MOST COMPREHENSIVE EDITION; and COMMONITORIUM ADVERSUS PROFANUS OMNIUM HAERETICORUM NOVITATES by Vincentius Lirinensis, as well as *a booke which He writt in June 1622 of many miracles of Gods punishments on those who contemned him in his saincts & of his fauours to others who honored him by honoring them, all then lately hapned in Northwales.*

John Hughes had registered as a student at the Seminarium Anglicum in 1636, and after seven years of studying had been ordained priest at the Basilica Lateranensi in Rome. The *Liber Ruber* of the college describes him as a man of remarkable patience and excellent behaviour (*vir patientiae singularis egregie se gessit),* and reports that he left for England on 28 September 1643 to serve as a secular priest. Five years later he decided to join the Jesuit movement and attended their centre at Watten, near St Omer, so as to enable him to participate in the St Francis Xavier Mission. He was stationed at Cwm, Llanrhyddol, and later at the Residence of St Winifred, with his headquarters at Holywell in the diocese of St Asaph, whose bishop at that time was his cousin, George Griffith of Garreg-lwyd. The superior of the Residence was William Morgan. When he was imprisoned in 1679, John Hughes was entrusted with his duties as superior. Hughes kept a record (Stonyhurst A.11) of the pilgrims who had sought cure for illnesses at Ffynnon Gwenfrewi. They came from far afield from such places as Perth-hir, Llanfoist, Welsh Newton, Werngochyn in Gwent, Manafon and Guilsfield in Montgomery, Erbistoc, St Asaph, Henllan, Denbigh, Llansant-ffraid, Conwy, Llanddona in Anglesey, Caernarfon, Llanfachreth, Cydweli and Amestree and Rotherwas in Herefordshire.

But John Hughes is known first and foremost for his editing and writing. In 1684 he edited and published his father's translation of DE IMITATIONE CHRISTI. The title-page reads: *Dilyniad Christ a elwir yn gyffredin Thomas a Kempis, Gwedi ei gyfieithu'n Gymraec ers talm o amser yn ol Editiwn yr Awdur gan Huw Owen, Gwenynog ym Môn, Esq;, Llundain, Gwedi ei imprintio ar gôst I.H. MDCLXXXIV.* The original manuscript of DE IMITATIONE CHRISTI, written by Thomas à Kempis himself in 1441, is kept in the Brussels Library. Heribertus Rosweydus published exact copies of this in 1617 and 1627. The title page reads: *Thomas A Kempis Canonici Regularis Ord. S. Avgvstini De Imitatione Christi, Libro Qvatuor Denuo ad fidem autographi anni M.CCCCXL1 recensiti Cum Vita eiusdem Thomae per Heribertvm Ros-vveydvm Societatis Iesv.* The phrase *Denuo ad fidem autographi* appears translated on the Welsh title-page thus: *yn ol Editiwn yr Awdur*. Hugh Owen himself wrote the preamble *Y Cyfieithydd at y Cymro mwynlan*. In it he refers to the doubts that existed concerning the authorship of DE IMITATIONE CHRISTI, refers to the arguments that finally prevailed about who truly wrote the work and the reasons given by Rosweydus for attributing it to Thomas à Kempis. These reasons were also published by Rosweydus: CERTISSIMA TESTIMONIA QUIBUS THOMAE A KEMPIS AUCTOR ASSERITUR LIBRORUM DE IMITATIONE CHRISTI. According to Hugh Owen the work had been wrongly ascribed in earlier editions to Joan Gerson of Paris, and also to Joan Gersen or Gassen of Germany.

English translations of these earlier editions appeared in 1502 and 1504. Richard Whitford, a native of Flintshire, published five editions of his English translation anonymously, although his name does appear on the 1556 edition. A Spanish translation was published as early as 1482. Other translations in French, Italian and Dutch followed.

Hugh Owen called his translation DILYNIAD CHRIST, an exact translation of the title that appeared on Richard Whitford's 1556 edition: FOLLOWING OF CHRIST. Another Welsh translation, attributed to *W.M.*, was published in Chester in 1723 with the title PATTRWM Y GWIR GRISTION NEU DDILYNIAD IESU GRIST. A second edition of this translation, wrongly attributed to Hugh Owen, was published in Shrewsbury in 1730.

As the title of Hugh Owen's translation suggests, DILYNIAD CHRIST is a moral treatise. Its 448 pages are divided into four chapters: warnings on the importance of living spiritually; remarks concerning man's inner life; concerning spiritual comfort; and concerning the Holy Sacrament.

Hugh Owen coined many a new word, such as *angelol, dirgeleddus* and *gostyngeiddio*. He probably got the word *dilyniad* from John Davies's DICTION-ARIUM DUPLEX, where it is given the Latin equivalent *immitatio*. Saunders Lewis applauds the translation:

Huw Owen kept faithfully to the Latin, to the technical terms of the Latin, to the figures of speech and the rhythms of Thomas à Kempis and close to the mind of the author from beginning to end. He deserves a place of honour amongst translators of the Renaissance period. Certainly there are mistakes in his language, in his mutations, in his constructions, and these not infrequent.

DILYNIAD CHRIST was published in 1684, forty years after Hugh Owen's death. His son John Hughes probably delayed the publication simply because at that time there were three other Welsh translations of this work in manuscript form in circulation amongst the Catholic faithful. John Hughes as editor, in his introduction to his father's translation, names the three translators. One of them was the Benedictine, Mathew Turbervil alias Humfredus Turbervil alias Eduardus Basset, a member of a staunch recusant family of Pen-llin in the Vale of Glamorgan, who was admitted to the English College at Valladolid in 1602. He served on the mission and was imprisoned for recusancy in Newgate prison and later in Wisbech, but was released. He returned to Glamorgan, where he died in 1645. Another of the translators was the Jesuit Thomas Jeffreyes (1591–1654) of Llechwedd Isaf, near Aberconwy, who joined the

Welsh Mission in 1625 and is known to have taught the children of recusant families in Monmouthshire and Breconshire between 1623 and 1644. The third translator was the secular priest Huw Parry alias Hugh Salisbury (1589–1660) from Flintshire, who was educated at Rome and Douai and served as a secular priest in north Wales. Unfortunately none of their translations has survived.

According to John Hughes his father also translated *the latest and most complete edition . . . of* THE BOOK OF RESOLUTION by Robert Persons. The final authentic edition of the book known earlier as THE BOOK OF RESOLUTION was A CHRISTIAN DIRECTORIE GUIDING MEN IN THEIR SALUATION, which appeared at St Omer in 1585. But in 1590 an edition *anomymously adapted from A Christian Directory for the use of protestants* and falsely attributed to Robert Persons was published, entitled THE SECOND PARTE OF THE BOOKE OF CHRISTIAN DIRECTORIE GUIDING MEN TO THEIR SALUA-TION, WRITTEN BY THE FORMER AUTHOR R.P. At the Cardiff Central Library there are remnants of a Welsh translation bearing the title DIRECTORI CHRIST-NOGOL in the hand of John Hughes. These remnants are translations of extracts from both the above volumes. Hugh Owen must have been misled by the fictitious reference *to the former author R.P.,* which appeared on the cover of the revised Protestant edition. We must conclude that John Hughes made copies of his father's translation to provide reading material for his Catholic followers. Indeed, he himself, in his manual ALLWYDD PARADWYS, instructs the head of the family when conducting morning prayers to read a chapter from DIRECTORI CHRISTNOGOL – *Pennod neu Wers o'r Directori Christianogol.*

According to John Hughes his father began translating religious treatises when he had barely reached his twenty-seventh year. This suggests that Hugh Owen's third translation, LIBELLUS VERE AUREUS, by Vincentius Lirinensis, was completed sometime later than 1602. The only Welsh translation of this work that has survived (Cwrtmawr 16) carries the date 1591 and is definitely the work of a mature Welsh scholar who was fully aware of Welsh literary trends in the mid-seventeenth century. The full title of the Welsh version reads:

Llyfr prydferth o waith Vincentius, ffranc, monach ac offeiriad o ynys Lirin, ynghweryl henafiaeth a gwirionedd y ffydd gatholic, yn erbyn newyddiaeth pob heresi, a wnaethpwyd er ys mwy noc un cant ar ddeg o flynyddoedd. Heb gynwys ynddo ddim ond a ddysgasai ynteu y gan henaduriaid, cyn no hynny o sancteiddiol enw, fal y dengys y llyfr ei hûn wrth ei ddarllen; ac yn awr wedi ei gyfieithu o'r Lladin i'r iaith Gamberaec, heb newidio dim o synwyr a deall ei araith, neu ei ymadrodd: er na allwyd hynny air yngair, ond nessaf y gallwyd trwy gadw priodoldeb y iaith Gamberaec, er mwyn denu ac annog y Cymru truain i ymgais a chyrchu at yr hên ffydd gatholic eu henafiaid. 1591.

(A beautiful book composed by Vincentius, a Frenchman, a monk and a priest from the Island of Lerins in the cause of the antiquity and the truth of the Catholic Faith against unfounded heresies, written eleven hundred years ago. Containing nothing but what he himself had learnt from the earlier elders renowned for their sanctity, as the book itself, when read, shows; and now translated from the Latin into the Welsh language, without changing the meaning of his words or sentences: although this was not possible word for word, but as near as possible yet retaining the correct idiom of the Welsh language, so as to attract and encourage the wretched Welsh people to endeavour to return to the old Catholic Faith of their forefathers.)

The date 1591 was the publication date of VINCENTII LIRINENSIS GALLI PRO CATHOLICAE FIDEI ANTIQVITATE

& VERITATE ADVERSUS PROPHANAS OMNIUM HAERESEON NOUATIONES, LIBELLUS VERE AUREUS, which suggests that this was the text that the translator used. Earlier Latin editions were printed in 1552 and 1586. There are slight variations in the Welsh translation, and one additional comment not found in the original Latin or in the English translation, THE GOLDEN TREATISE OF THE ANTIENT AND LEARNED FATHER . . . TRANSLATED INTO ENGLISH BY A.P. 1651, which proves that it was the work of an ardent recusant:

Y tri phwngc y mae yn dir i bob dyn eu cadw yn ddyfal os ch[w]ennych na'i alw'n Gatholic, na pharhau yn ffydd yr Eglwys Gatholic allan o'r hon nid oes nac iechydwriaeth i berchen enaid, na chadwedigaeth i'w ddisgwyl.

(These are the three principles which every man must diligently accept, if one wishes to be acknowledged as a Catholic and remain faithful to the Catholic Church, if excluded, there is no salvation to anyone's soul nor any deliverance in the offing.)

It will be noted that he uses the word *iechydwriaeth*, a word first used by William Salesbury in his Welsh version of the Anglican BOOK OF COMMON PRAYER (*Llyfr Gweddi Gyffredin*), 1567.

LLYFR PRYDFERTH O WAITH VINCENTIUS (Cwrtmawr 16) and another translation, CRYNODEB CATECHISM DOWAY WEDI EI GYMHWYSO AT GYRHAEDDIAD PLANT A RHAI DILEN (Cwrtmawr 15), were transcribed by the same person. The latter is a translation of extracts from AN ABSTRACT OF THE DOUAY CATECHISM (Douai, 1697) and from the original catechism AN ABRIDGEMENT OF CHRISTIAN DOCTRINE, which Henry Turberville published in Douai in 1649 primarily for use at Douai College. It contains not only a catechism but also a series of daily devotions and good thoughts for every day of the week, in simple, unaffected language.

John Hughes returned to Wales in 1643 strongly aware that Welsh devotional manuals were very scarce. He waited for some time, hoping that one of his fellow missionary priests would produce one. However, having waited in vain for some thirty years, he decided to compile his own, for the benefit of his *dear Brothers and Sisters and my other faithful Friends in Gwent and Breconshire*, and published it in 1670: ALLWYDD NEU AGORIAD PARADWYS I'R CYMRY, HYNNY YW GWEDDIAU, DEVOTIONAU, CYNGHORION AC ATHRAWIAETHAU TRA DUWIOL YN MYNNU AGORYD Y PORTH A MYNED I MEWN I'R NEF, WEDI EU CYNNULL O AMRYW LYFRAU DUWIOL, A'I CYFANSODDI GAN I.H. YN LVYCK. IMPRINTIWYD YN Y FLWYDDYN M DC LXX (*Key to Paradise for the Welsh people, that is Prayers, Devotions, Instructions and godly Doctrines seeking to open the Gate to go to Heaven, collecting from many godly books and compiled by I.H.*). The imprint Lyuck (Liège) is fictitious: the manual was actually printed in London. As the title-page indicates, the manual is a collection of prayers, devotions, instructions and doctrinal tenets. In the preface Hughes acknowledges his indebtedness to THE KEY OF PARADISE by John Wilson, and attributes the section entitled *Guide to those guilty of deadly sins* to Charles Baker *alias* David Lewis, who was martyred in 1679. A glossary of unfamiliar Welsh words appears as an appendix, together with notes on the pronunciation of Latin for the sake of the English *who pronounce Latine extremely falsly*.

ALLWYDD PARADWYS, with some omissions and some additional prayers, including *Psallwyr Iesu*, appeared in the manual entitled ALLWYDD Y NEF, which was published in London in 1776. The editor was David Gregory Powel (Dewi Nant Brân), a Catholic priest who was born in Llanfihangel Nant Brân. He was a member of the Franciscan Order and served in the homes of Catholics in parishes as far apart as Defynnog in west Breconshire and Chepstow. In the preface, *Y Rhaglith At y Cymry Ffyddlon*, he explains why he was publishing the Welsh manual:

Mae rwôn wedi cant o flynyddoedd er pan argraffwyd llyfr Allwydd Paradwys yn gwlad yr Ellmyn, trwy haelioni, cymwynasgarwch, traul a charedigrwydd rhai o'r Saison ffyddlon at genedl a iaith y Cymry. A gan fod yr un llyfr ysprydol wedi mynd yn brin, yn anaml iawn ac yn anhawdd i'w gael, er addysg ac adeiladaeth, er cyssur a diddanwch, er daioni a lles ysprydol i eneidiau'r ffyddloniaid o'r tair talaith, bwriadais gyflawni hynny o ddiffyg, yn enwedig, pan clowais bagad ohonoch yn dymuno cael y cyfryw weddiau yn eich iaith eich hun.

(A hundred years have now passed since the publication of Allwydd Paradwys *in the land of the Germans, through the generosity, beneficence, donations and kindness of some of the faithful English towards the Welsh nation and the language. And because the only spiritual book had become scarce, and very rare and difficult to come by for educational and edifying purposes, for comfort and entertainment and for the spiritual benefit of the faithful souls in the three regions, I decided to meet this need, especially when I heard that many of you wished to have such prayers in your own language.)*

The manual includes two hymns of his own composition. One of them, entitled *Te lucis ante terminum*, opens with these verses:

Cyn tywyll nos, O Arglwydd Nef,
Â dyfal lef o'r galon,
Erchwn arnat, Geidwad cu,
I'n cadw rhag peryglon.

Cilied ffyrdd pob breuddwyd ffôl.
A phob gwag eilun feddwl.
Rhag pydredd corff, O! gwared ni,
Gorthrecha'r gelyn gwbwl. etc.

(Before the dark night, O Lord of Heaven, with earnest cry from the heart, we beg of you, Dear Saviour, to keep us from dangers. Let the ways of foolish dreams pass away and all vain imaginations. From the corruptive body, O! save us. Vanquish the enemy.)

David Gregory Powell also translated and published two catechisms:

CATHECHISM BYRR O'R ATHRAWIAETH GHRISTNOGOL; ER ADDYSG YSPRYDOL I BLANT A'R WERINOS ANWYBODUS TRWY GYMRU OLL, Llundain, 1764.

SAIL YR ATHRAWIAETH GATHOLIG, GYNNWYSEDIG MEWN PROFESS FFYDD A GYHOEDDWYD GAN PIWS Y BEDWERYDD; AR WEDD HOLIAD AC ATTEB, A GYFIEITHWYD ER LLES I'R CYMRY, Llundain, 1764, 2nd edition 1835.

Gwilym Pugh of Penrhyn held a captain's commission in the Royalist army at Raglan Castle during the Civil War. But in 1660 he joined the Benedictine Order at St Edmund's, Paris. Two manuscripts (NLW 4710B and 13167B) in his hand have survived. According to the dates found on the frontispieces of these, they were copied for the most part during his days as a student in the English College at Valladolid, from 1670 to 1677, which suggests that some of the contents were composed in preparation for his return to Wales on the mission. He settled in Gwent in Blackbrook, the home of the Bodenham family, serving the Catholic faithful in the area and following his profession as a country physician. His compositions included two translations from English, Pllaswyr Iessv and Erfynnion nev Littaniav Evraid, and one original bilingual catechism in Latin and Welsh, entitled Crynodeb or Athrawiaeth Gristnogawl.

The original English of Pllaswyr Iessv was first printed in 1529 and entitled An invocacyon gloryous named ye psalter of Jesus. A new edition appeared in 1575, this time bearing the title Certain deuout and Godly petitions, commonly called Iesus Psalter. It was a very popular manual of devotions, as evidenced by the fact that at least fourteen editions appeared before the end of the century. It was called Psalter, as it contained 150 petitions, the number of the psalms in the OT Psalter. The distinctive feature of the style of the English original is the rhythm and the assonances of the lines and the ever-recurring rhyme chiefly using 'me' and 'thee'. Gwilym Pugh pays little attention to these features in his free translation, as this quotation shows (the orthography is standardized, for that of Gwilym Pugh is an enigma):

Trugarha wrth bechaduriaid oll, Iesu, rwy'n atolwg i Ti,
Tro eu gwydiau nhwy i rinweddau.
Gwna nhwy yn gyflawnwyr cywir o'th gyfraith di a'th serchog hoffwyr di.
Arwain ny-nhw i ddedwyddwch yn y gogoniant tragwyddawl.
Trugarha hefyd wrth yr eneidiau yn y purdan,
Er mwyn dy chwerw-dost ddioddefaint, rwyf i yn atolwg, Iesu,
O Santaidd Drindod, vn unig wir Dduw, trugarha wrthym.

(Have mercy on all sinners. Jesus, I beg of you,
Change their sins into virtues.
Make them true observers of your law and your loving devotees.
Lead them to bliss in the eternal glory.
Have mercy also on those souls in purgatory,
For the sake of your cruel suffering, I beg you, Jesus,
O Holy Trinity, the only true God, have mercy on me.)

ERFYNNION NEV LITTANIAV EVRAID is a translation of
THE GOLDEN LETANY IN ENGLISH, by R. Copland
(1531). Various editions of it appeared, some incor-
porated in manuals such as CERTAINE DEVOUT AND
GODLY PETITIONS (1596) and MANUAL OF PRAYERS
(Roven, 1613 and Paris, 1630). These are the opening
lines of Gwilym Pugh's translation (again, the orthography is standardized):

Arglwydd, trugarha wrthym ni,
Christ, trugarha wrthym ni,
Arglwydd, trugarha wrthym ni, a rho i ni rinwedd
A meddwl o enaid ar y ddaear i allu dy wasanaethu di
Ac uwchlaw'r ddaear yn ôl bodd dy galon di.
Duw tragwyddawl Dad, er dy nefawl rinwedd di, trugarha
wrthym ni.
Mab Duw, pryniawdwr y byd, trugarha wrthym ni,
Duw digreuedig, aneilltol Drindod, trugarha wrthym ni
Er dy naturiaeth ddwyfol, trugarha wrthym ni,
Er dy anherfynawl larieidd, trugarha wrthym ni.

(Lord, have mercy on us,
Christ, have mercy on us,
Lord, have mercy on us, and grant us virtue
And awareness of one's soul on earth to enable us to serve you
And above the earth according to your heart's delight.
God the eternal Father, for the sake of your heavenly virtue,
have mercy on us.
Son of God, saviour of the world, have mercy on us.

Uncreated God, undivided Trinity, have mercy on us.
For the sake of your divine nature, have mercy on us.
For the sake of your unending generosity, have mercy on us.)

The full title of Gwilym Pugh's Welsh catechism reads: CRYNODEB OR ATHRAWIAETH GRISTNOGAWL SUDD O WAITH GWILYM PUE . . . PWY BYNAG A FUNN FOD YN SAFIEDIG, O FLAEN HOLL BETHAU MAY YN ANGENRHEIDIOL IDDO FO DDAL Y FFUDD GATHOLIG. (*Christian Doctrine composed by Gwilym Pue . . . whoever wants to be saved, above all it is necessary for him to hold on to the Catholic Faith*). The title of the Latin version reads: ENCHIRIDIUM CHATECHISTICUM SIVE CHATECHISMUS PRO PVERIS SCHOLARIBUS AUTHORE F.G.P. (*Cathechistal Manual or Catechism for Schoolboys Author F.G.P.*), and the date of composition is added: '1676'. For content he appears to be indebted to Richard Vaughan's EGLVRHAD HELAETH-LAWN (1618), but his Welsh, orthographically and lexically, bears little resemblance to that which was acceptable in his day. He prefers antiquated words and avoids English derivatives.

His manuscripts contain numerous dogmatic poems of his own composition. In his opinion poems other than religious ones were nothing but vanity. He composed *awdlau, cywyddau* and *englynion* on such subjects as the life of Christ and Mary, the Holy Ghost, the Mass and the *Miserere*, and the *Magnificat*. One of the *cywyddau, Buchedd ein Harglwydd Iessu Grist*, is 2,000 lines long. He is familiar with these metrical forms, but his *cynganeddion* are faulty. His lines are alliterated but not according to the strict rules of *cynghanedd*. In spite of many faults, his literary style is traditionally bardic, as illustrated by these lines:

Pwy draw a geir mor drugarog
Ag yw'r gŵr sydd ar y grog?
Pwy ond Duw? Pwy edwyn y dyn
A roi aelod er i elyn.
Crist yn gryf ar y groes
Eron ni rhoes ei einioes . . .

(Is there anyone as merciful as the man who is on the cross?
Who other than God? Does anyone know of any man who
would give his limb for his enemy's sake. Christ, strong on the
cross, gave his life for us.)

His *Buchedd Gwenn Frewu Santes* ('Life of Saint
Winifred'), which he composed in his old age, has
been written in the popular folk metrical form
known as *mesur tri thrawiad,* a metre with three
rhymes in every couplet, and the second and last line
rhyming and formulated in *cynghanedd sain.* But the
metre in his poem is bereft of *cynghanedd sain,* as this
verse, which opens in the traditional way by inviting
listeners, indicates:

Dowch ataf fi y bobol, gwrandewch chwi gewch garol
O ystyr rhagorol i'w draethu,
Cerdd sydd o rinwedd o'r dechref i'r diwedd.
Yn hon cewch chi fuchedd Gwenfrewy.

(Come near me, my people, listen, you'll hear a meaningful
carol worth reciting, a virtuous poem from beginning to end in
which you will find the life of Winifred.)

His other poem, *Buchedd Martyn Luther, yr Apostat*
('Life of Martin Luther, Apostate'), is in a different
but equally popular free metrical form known as
mesur triban. After an onslaught on Luther's character, he warns the reader to remain loyal to the
Mother Church:

> Gad yr anghenfil, rhag cael cam,
> Glyn wrth dy Fam, yr Eglwys.

(Desert the Monster lest you be unfairly treated. Cling to your Mother, the Church.)

One gathers from illustrations in his manuscripts that Gwilym Pugh, like the martyred missionary priest Philip Evans, was a harpist. He composed verses in 1648 prognosticating the end of the rule of the Roundheads and the return of the King and the Mass: *messurau yw Datcanv gida'r Delyn* ('verses to be sung to harp accompaniment'). His *Carol Nadolig* cannot be described as being Catholic and would probably be particularly welcomed by all Christian sects:

> Dewch i bererina
>   Yn barod gyda ni
> I Fethlehem pan ar eira,
>   Lle ganed vn i ni.
> Lle mae bara yr angyliaid
>   Gwedi ei ddwyn
>   Yn ymborth mwyn
> A'i roi mewn preseb y nifeiliaid.
>
> Y tri bugail gwirion
>   Wrth wadd angylion cad
> Yn mynd i Fethlem dirion
>   I addoli y Mab rhad.
> Cawn ninnau fawl a gwawd i'n Naf
>   O'r nef y doeth
>   Ei eni yn noeth.
> Y person ail sy Dduw goruchaf.
>
> I'r Tad yn yr uchelder
>   Y bytho moliant mawr,
> I'r Mab yr hwn i'r ddaear
>   O'r nef a ddoeth i lawr,

Ag i'r Yspryd Glân, bid moliant
I vn Duw Tri
Oddi wrth nyni
Y bytho clod a mawr ogoniant.

(Come with us now on a pilgrimage to Bethlehem, while it snows, to the spot where this one was born for our sake, where angelic bread has been brought as good food and placed in a manger for animals.

The three innocent shepherds at the invitation of angels were found going to delightful Bethlehem to worship the gift of a Son. We shall hear heavenly praises to our Lord. From heaven he came, born naked, second person who is God Most High.

To the Father in the highest may there be great praise, to the Son who came down to earth from heaven, and to the Holy Ghost, let there be praise, to the three in one God, from us let there be praise and great glory.)

His manuscripts also contain *cywyddau* depicting the history of his recusant family, as in *Panegyris Penrhynniana* or *Llwyrwys Penrhyn a'i mawl*, and his own personal relationships, as in *Bardd Nad Gwilym am ei dad Phylip Pue* and *Mawl i Morgan Gwynn o Daliarus ag o wadd i fod yn Gatholig*. There are also *awdlau* concerning the Civil War, such as *Awdl llu Siarls 2* or *Brenhin pan ddoyth ef a llu or Yscottiaid i Gaerfrangon*.

We also find in his manuscript copies of Gruffydd Robert's *Englynion y Pader, yr Ave Maria a'r Gred*, Richard White's carols (*Pymp Carolay Mr White*), and poems by his Catholic acquaintances, especially John Jones (Siôn Siones), whom he describes as a recusant (*vir sane catholicus*) from Breconshire (*eius Patria Breconia*), an area known for its recusancy. According to the records there were 164 known recusants in the county in 1676. One of John Jones's poems, dated

1676, is entitled *Gwrthnebrwydd Rhyng y Calfyniaed ar Chatholygiaed Mewn Pynciae Ffydd* ('The dispute between the Calvinists and Catholics on matters of Faith'). He refers to all the usual *puncta Fidei* found in the catechisms: *Rheol ein teidiau (Traditiones), Bibyl (Scriptura), Ffydd Pedr (Auctoritas Ecclesiae), Pabau (De Summo Pontifice), Gollwng pechode (Remissio Peccatorum), Y Gyffes (De Confessione), Y Saint (De Invocatione Sanctorum), Haeddiant (De Merito), Esgyrn (De Reliquiis), Altriad (De Transubstantione), Olew (De Extrema Unction), Offeiriaid Diwreigi (Coelibes), Purdan (De Purgatorio), Lluniau (De Imaginibus)* and *Yn erbyn y Nefoedd (Obstinatio)*. But he depends on Biblical references for his proofs.

The metrical form used is the popular *mesur tri thrawiad*. There are twenty-seven four-lined verses, each couplet having the same rhyme, and in the first he invites the Calvinists – that is, the Anglicans – to listen:

> *Gwŷr gauffydd digyffro, dowch ataf i wrando,*
> *Bob rhai sy'n gofalio ar eneidie.*
> *Mi a agora i chwi 'chydig o'r pyncie arbennig*
> *Sydd rhyng y chatholig a chwithe.*
>
> *(You apathetic heretics, come near me to listen,*
> *All who care for the souls,*
> *I will explain some differences of Faith*
> *That exist between the catholic and you.)*

Gwilym Pugh apologizes for the defects in the author's Welsh and for the English words he uses, such as *marccio, tincer, gwarante, altriad, prwfie, example* and so on.

Another poem attributed to John Jones is to be found

in NLW 10893E 15, entitled *Trybane . . . holl ddisgid-iaeth gwreiddie'r Ffydd.* Its penultimate verse reads:

> *Os gofyn neb yn vnlle*
> *Pwy ganodd y tribanne,*
> *Un John Jones, ni chredid fe*
> *nes prwfo'r pwncke yn ole.*

(If anyone anywhere asks who composed the tribannau, some John Jones. He was not believed until all subjects were clarified.)

It is a long poem of 223 verses in dialogue form between a Protestant and a Catholic. Catholic dogma is discussed with special reference to such controversial subjects as *Delwe* (*De Imaginibus*), *Mair . . . yn fendigedig* (*Conceptio Immaculata*), *Ymprydio* (*De Ieiunio*), *Ymswyno wrth y groes* (*De Veneratione Crucis*), *Antichrist* (*Antichrist*), *Y bara yn fywiol gnawd* (*De Transubstantione*), *Ni byddi byth gadwedig heb fod mewn ffydd Gatholig* (*Auctoritas Ecclesiae*), *Tradition* (*Traditiones*), *Ni all ffydd Pedr ffaelu* (*De Summo Pontifice*) and *Na wrthod ffydd rhag carchar* (*Obstinatio*).

Gwilym Pugh's manuscripts also contain ten *cywyddau* by Siôn Cent, a *cywydd* entitled *Yr Aberth Bendigaid* (The Holy Mass) by Edward Turberville, and *Yr Awdwl Bigog* by Edward Dafydd (Edward Bach), a recusant from Trefddyn, near Pontypool, Gwent, who died in 1662. Professor R. Geraint Gruffydd edited the poem in LLÊN CYMRU (1959) with the title *Awdl Wrthryfelgar*, and gave ample evidence that the poem dealt with the attempt of the earl of Essex to raise the citizens of London against the government, an uprising that Edward Dafydd obviously supported and wanted all Wales to support. In the event, Essex was proclaimed traitor, sentenced to death and executed on 23 February 1601. Edward Bach also composed numerous religious *cwndidau* in the metrical form known as *awdl-gywydd*, a *cywydd deuair hirion* and some *englynion*, all testifying to his competence in handling the popular metrical forms of the period and to his familiarity with the traditional poetic genres. The Gwent dialect bearing the usual signs of Anglicization is used with pride, and his Catholic commitment is evident enough throughout. His *cywydd* celebrates the victorious entry into London of General George Monck in 1660 and the restoration of Charles II. These are the opening lines of his *Christmas Carol*:

> *Gressor yr gayaf glas y frigg*
> *ar gwyl nydolig ffrwythlon.*
> *Gresso glywed pob dûn syw*
> *yn gofyn rhyw newyddion.*
> *Gresso yr amser hunn y kad*
> *o wrthey/r/ tad dirgelion*
> *fab ay eni o forwyn wenn*
> *yn geidwad penn myddygon.*

(Welcome to evergreen winter and the fruitful Christmas festivity. Welcome to hearing that every wise man seeks some news. Welcome to this occasion when, following the miracles of the father of mysteries, a son was born of a holy virgin as a saviour, chief of physicians.)

The printing of Catholic books had been prohibited since the early days of Elizabeth's reign, and the adverse effect this had on Catholic writings and the ability of the Catholics to campaign through the Welsh language for their faith cannot be over-estimated. However, the annually renewed Act that prohibited the printing of Catholic books was not renewed in 1695. By that time the Catholic mission in Wales had long lost its impetus, especially after the martyrdom of the Welshmen Philip Evans and David Lewis in 1680. Whereas in 1644 there were twenty-four Jesuit missionary priests active in the Districts of St Francis Xavier and St Winifred, by 1678 they had been reduced to ten, and the secular priests and the Benedictines were fewer still.

The Toleration Act of 1689 brought no relief to *any papist or popish recusant*. In 1700 a reward of £100 was fixed for anybody who informed the authorities of anyone saying Mass, and it was decreed that any person who had not become an Anglican by the time he was eighteen would be disinherited, and that families who sent children abroad to be educated would be fined £100. By then the government and the Anglican establishment were not their only opponents. The new Puritan dissenters were also by then a sect to contend with, as were the Methodists later. It is no surprise that no Catholic writings have been found in any manuscripts later than 1676, the date of Gwilym Pugh's manuscripts, and none appeared in print for almost a century after the publishing of DILYNIAD CHRIST in 1684 until the appearance of David Gregory Powell's two cate-chisms in 1764 and his ALLWYDD Y NÊF in 1771.

A Select Bibliography

A. E. Allison and D. M. Rogers, THE CONTEMPORARY PRINTED LITERATURE OF THE ENGLISH COUNTER-REFORMATION BETWEEN 1558 AND 1640, 2 vols., Aldershot, 1989–94.

A. C. Beales, EDUCATION UNDER PENALTY, London, 1963.

H. N. Birt, OBIT BOOK OF THE ENGLISH BENEDICTINES, 1913.

Geraint Bowen (ed.), Y DRYCH KRISTNOGAWL, Caerdydd, 1997.

Idem (ed.), GWSSANAETH Y GWŶR NEWYDD, Caerdydd, 1970.

Idem, 'Robert Gwyn o Benyberth, Awdur Catholig', TRANSACTIONS OF THE HONOURABLE SOCIETY OF CYMMRODORION [THSC], 1996, 33.

Idem, 'Allwydd neu Agoriad Paradwys i'r Cymrv, John Hughes, 1670', THSC, 1961, 88.

Idem, 'Catholigion Cymru yn Oes William Morgan', in Glanmor Williams et al., WILLIAM MORGAN, Y DYN, EI GYFNOD A'I FEIBL, Yr Wyddgrug, 1988, 31–56.

Idem, 'Siôn Dafydd Rhys ac Institutiones', LLÊN CYMRU, XI, 1998, 38.

Martin Cleary, 'The Catholic Resistance in Wales, 1568–1678', BLACKFRIARS, March 1957.

Henry Foley, RECORDS OF THE ENGLISH PROVINCE OF THE SOCIETY OF JESUS, London, 1877.

T. Gwynfor Griffith, 'De Italica Pronunciatione', ITALIAN STUDIES, VIII, 1953, 71.

R. Geraint Gruffydd (ed.), A GUIDE TO WELSH LITERATURE, c.1530–1700, Cardiff, 1997.

Idem, ARGRAFFWYR CYNTAF CYMRU: GWASGAU DIRGEL Y CATHOLIGION, Caerdydd, 1972.

Idem, 'Cywydd, Englynion a Chwndidau gan Edward Dafydd o Drefddyn', LLÊN CYMRU, XI, 1998, 213.

E. Gwynne Jones, CYMRU A'R HEN FFYDD, Caerdydd, 1951.

Thomas Parry, THEATER DV MOND SEF IVV GORSEDD Y BYD, Rhosier Smyth, Caerdydd, 1930.

Siôn Dafydd Rhys, CAMBROBRYTANNICAE CYMRAEC-AEVE LINGUAE INSTITUTIONES ET RUDIMENTA, London, 1592.

D. M. Rogers, Y DRYCH CRISTNOGAWL, Menston, 1972.

Idem, ATHRAVAETH GRISTNOGAWL, Morys Clynnog, Menston, 1972.

Idem, EGLVRHAD HELAETH-LAWN ROBERT BELLARMIN, Menston, 1972.

John Ryan, 'Sources of the Tradition of the Catechism of St Peter Canisius', JOURNAL OF THE WELSH BIBLIOGRAPHICAL SOCIETY, 11, 225.

A. C. Southern, ELIZABETHAN RECUSANT PROSE, London, 1950.

D. Aneurin Thomas, THE WELSH ELIZABETHAN CATHOLIC MARTYRS, Cardiff, 1971.

E. H. Wilkins, A HISTORY OF ITALIAN LITERATURE, Oxford, 1954.

G. J. Williams (ed.), GRAMADEG CYMRAEG GAN GRUFFYDD ROBERT, Caerdydd, 1939.

The Author

Geraint Bowen was born in Llanelli in 1915 and educated at Aberaeron Grammar School and University College, Cardiff, where he took his master's degree and doctorate. He won the Chair at the 1946 National Eisteddfod of Wales. He taught at Ruabon Grammar School from 1947 until 1961 and was appointed HM Inspector of Schools. From 1975 until 1977 he edited Y FANER and he was appointed Archdruid of Wales in 1978 and visiting professor at Ottawa University in 1983. He has edited Y TRADDODIAD RHYDDIAITH (3 vols), YSGRIFENNU CREADIGOL, Y DRYCH KRISTNOGAWL, Y GWAREIDDIAD CELTAIDD, and ATLAS MEIRIONNYDD; and his publications include HANES GORSEDD Y BEIRDD (joint author), GOLWG AR ORSEDD Y BEIRDD, BRO A BYWYD W. J. GRUFFYDD, BWYD LLWY O BADELL AWEN (*A Manual on Welsh Metrics*), a biography, O GROTH Y DDAEAR, and a volume of collected poems, CERDDI.

Designed by Jeff Clements
Typesetting at the University of Wales Press in
11pt Palatino and printed in Great Britain by
Dinefwr Press, Llandybïe, 1999

British Library Cataloguing in Publication Data.
A catalogue record for this book is available from the
British Library.

ISBN 0-7083-1515-1

The Publishers wish to acknowledge the financial
assistance of the Arts Council of Wales towards the cost
of producing this volume.